**this book is from
the kitchen library of**

_____

ALSO BY ART GINSBURG, MR. FOOD®

The Mr. Food® Cookbook, OOH it's so GOOD!!™ (1990)

Mr. Food® Cooks Like Mama (1992)

Mr. Food® Cooks Chicken (1993)

Mr. Food® Cooks Pasta (1993)

Mr. Food® Makes Dessert (1993)

Mr. Food® Cooks Real American (1994)

Mr. Food®'s Favorite Cookies (1994)

Mr. Food® Grills It All in a Snap (1995)

Mr. Food®'s Fun Kitchen Tips and Shortcuts (and Recipes, Too!) (1995)

MR. FOOD®'S
Quick and Easy Side Dishes

Art Ginsburg
Mr. Food®

WILLIAM MORROW AND COMPANY, INC.

New York

Library of Congress Cataloging-in-Publication Data

Ginsburg, Art.
    Mr. Food®'s quick and easy side dishes / Art Ginsburg.
        p.   cm.
    Includes index.
    ISBN 0–688–13712–1
    1. Quick and easy cookery.   2. Side dishes (Cookery)   I. Title.
    II. Title: Mister Food's quick and easy side dishes.
    TX8323.5.G56   1995   94–39385
                                                                              CIP

Printed in the United States of America

First Edition

1 2 3 4 5 6 7 8 9 10

BOOK DESIGN BY MICHAEL MENDELSOHN / MM DESIGN 2000, INC.

Dedicated to
Dad–
My greatest influence

Acknowledgments

What a year this has been! We moved the whole MR. FOOD® team into a new home in South Florida, where we can really spread out and have more space to do our "thing"—which is cooking, cooking, and more cooking for my television shows and cookbooks!

The move and this book couldn't have happened without the constant support and incredible perseverance of my family and colleagues. Each of them played a vital part in making it all come together, and I'm extremely grateful to them all.

Once again, my daughter, Caryl Ginsburg Gershman, "Art"-fully pulled together my words and coordinated this entire project. And, once again, Howard Rosenthal shared his endless creativity in helping to develop and choose just the right recipes and helpful tips, making sure they work easily, time after time. My son, Steve Ginsburg, continues to lend all of us his experienced eye, and thanks to the creative input and computer wizardry of Roy Fantel, it was easier than ever to bring together all of this information.

Patty Rosenthal, Alice Palombo, Jean Suits, and Monique Drummond have stepped into their new recipe testing roles masterfully, and none of us would have gotten this far without the caring, attentive assistance of Marilyn Ruderman, Beth Ives, and Stacey Dempsey.

I wouldn't miss another opportunity to thank my agent, Bill Adler, and my ever-energetic publicist, Phyllis Heller. To my editor, Harriet Bell, and also to Al Marchioni, Skip Dye, Deborah Weiss

Geline, and Kathleen Hackett at William Morrow, I extend more thanks for top-notch work.

As I said before, the "thank-you mat" is out for Ethel, Chuck, and the rest of our growing family who are always there to give me the boosts I need. I really appreciate you guys.

My appreciation extends to the following companies and organizations, too, for their assistance in providing helpful information and product suggestions:

Chilean Fresh Fruit Association
Dairy Management Inc.
Idaho Potato Commission
McCormick®/Schilling®
The National Honey Board
The National Pasta Association
Produce Marketing Association
Sargento Cheese Co., Inc.
Western New York Apple Growers Association
Wisconsin Milk Marketing Board
U.S.A. Rice Council

Contents

Introduction

As I travel around the country, I ask my viewers and readers what they need the most help with in the kitchen. Time and time again they ask me, "After I decide on a main dish, I never know what to make *to go with it*. I've run out of ideas. Help!" So I came up with a book full of "go-along" ideas that I *know* will help.

Most people have a good selection of standard main dishes that they like to make over and over. So for dinner they fix their usual hamburgers, meat loaf, steak, chicken, fish, or pasta. But what else? Well, that's not a problem anymore! I've found just what you need for those times when you can't figure out what to make "**with** it"—all with the **full tastes from Mom's table**, but as **new** as today. . . . You know, **easy** and **no-fail**! Whether you're a seasoned veteran cook or a beginning cook, you'll be a **hero**!

I knew I needed to put together recipes that would, as do all of my recipes, use readily available ingredients right from your cupboard or off your supermarket shelves. They would have to be not only quick and easy, but also a little different—colorful and exciting dishes to add an extra spark to your table without much fuss.

And not only did I come up with over one hundred winning recipes for you—like Spaghetti Rice, the perfect chicken "go-along" (page 63), Sweet Potato Salad (page 135), Confetti Vegetable Salad (page 134), and even Pretzel Stuffing (page 124)—but I've also included some really helpful charts and information about each type of side-dish food. Well, just look at the Great Greens chapter. . . . It's got helpful hints on cleaning and topping your

greens, along with drawings to help you be adventurous in choosing new greens and mixing and matching them with each other and with different toppings.

In the Fruit Festival chapter, I've got some quick tips for fancy ways to cut and serve fresh fruit. (You never know when that little extra touch might make a world of difference!) Then, in other chapters, there are great pasta, potato, and rice cooking tips, and advice on storing your fresh veggies. And, for a change, I've put all this information at the *front* of the individual chapters. That way you've really got the help you need right at your fingertips.

So from now on . . . no more worries about what to make *"with it."* No more serving the same potato or rice dish over and over! Hooray! I can send you off to think of new questions to ask me— that is, if you have time while you're busy exploring all the Great Greens, Potato Pleasers, Rice to Entice, "Lotsa" Pasta, Vanishing Veggies, Hearty Hodgepodge, Bold Cold Salads, and the Fruit Festival that follow. I bet you'll get started right away with saying goodbye to boring side dishes, and hello to lots of tantalizing **OOH it's so GOOD!!**™

Introduction

Quick Measures

	Equals
Dash	Less than ⅛ teaspoon
3 teaspoons	1 tablespoon
4 tablespoons	¼ cup
5 tablespoons plus 1 teaspoon	⅓ cup
6 tablespoons	⅜ cup
8 tablespoons	½ cup
10 tablespoons plus 2 teaspoons	⅔ cup
12 tablespoons	¾ cup
16 tablespoons	1 cup
2 tablespoons	1 fluid ounce
1 cup	½ pint or 8 fluid ounces
2 cups	1 pint or 16 fluid ounces
4 cups	2 pints or 1 quart or 32 fluid ounces
4 quarts	1 gallon or 128 fluid ounces
2 tablespoons fat or butter	1 ounce
¼ pound (1 stick) butter	½ cup
½ pound butter	1 cup
Juice of 1 lemon	About 3 tablespoons
1 cup lemon juice	Juice of 4 to 6 lemons
Juice of 1 orange	About ½ cup
Grated peel of 1 lemon	About 1½ teaspoons
Grated peel of 1 orange	About 1 tablespoon

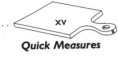

Notes from MR. FOOD®

Lighten Up . . .
with Cooking Sprays

Throughout this book, and in my other cookbooks, I frequently mention nonstick vegetable cooking spray and recommend using it to coat cookware and bakeware before placing food in or on them. Here's why—these sprays are easy to use, they add no measurable amount of fat to our food, and now they're even available in nonaerosol *and* in flavored varieties! The flavored sprays are super ways to add a touch of taste without adding fat and calories. So far I've tried them in butter, olive oil, garlic, mesquite, and Asian flavors. I think they do a great job of "greasing" *without* the grease.

Serving Sizes

The serving sizes listed in these recipes are all for side dish–sized portions, since side dishes are what this book is all about! I like to serve generous-sized portions myself, so I generally figure that way when I list the number of portions to expect from my recipes. Of course, many of these recipes can certainly be used as main-course dishes, as long as you keep in mind that they won't yield as many servings if used that way. Yes, appetites do vary and *you* know the special food loves of your eaters, so, as always, you be the judge of how many batches to make.

Packaged Foods

Packaged food sizes may vary by brand. Generally, the sizes indicated in these recipes are average sizes. If you can't find the exact package size listed in the ingredients, whatever package is closest in size will usually do the trick.

Great Greens

Salads used to be basic and, well, boring. . . .You know, a salad was a salad, with few options. Maybe we cut up some iceberg lettuce with a wedge of tomato and, for fancy times, we added some cucumbers and onions.

Today, with the advantages of sophisticated farming methods and modern transportation, salads are exciting, really exciting! And they aren't just served *before* dinner anymore. They are becoming part of the entire meal. You could say salads are the perfect side dish because they're colorful, easy, and good for us—and the options are endless.

I think we could safely say that great dressings make great salads. I mean, how much better is a bowl of crisp romaine lettuce with a rich Creamy Caesar Dressing (see page 21)? Or delicate spinach with a sweet, light, poppy seed dressing (like the one on page 13)? Dressing is the signature that makes "just a salad" into a "wow!" salad—and have I got some great ones here!

And there are other ways to "special up" the salad. On the following pages I'll show you some of the most popular greens available in the markets today, plus a listing of toppings that will accent any of them. Be adventurous and try different combinations to come up with some new favorites of your own.

So, mix 'em, match 'em, or dress 'em to satisfy your gang's taste buds—and before you know it, no meal will be complete without a salad on the side and an **OOH it's so GOOD!!**™ on your lips.

Great Greens

How to Choose Greens

There are so many greens available to us today! Here's a listing of the ones you'll find in our markets along with illustrations to help you identify them.

Boston Lettuce

A loosely packed lettuce with medium-sized green leaves. Very similar to Bibb lettuce, with Bibb being a bit more open and crinkly in shape. Both come in small-sized heads and have a tender texture that is complemented by delicate dressings.

Iceberg Lettuce

It's technically referred to as *crisp head lettuce*, but today most of us call it *iceberg*. Pale green with firmly packed leaves, it has a crunchy texture and is a bit blander than other varieties widely available now.

Leaf Lettuce

A loose-leafed variety with slightly tapered leaves that are either light green or red, depending on the variety. Its flavor and its curly ends make it great for both salads and garnish. (Ivy and oak are forms of leaf lettuce.)

Romaine

Deep green in color, with broad, tapered leaves, romaine is perfect for salads that need to stand up to strong dressings. Its leaf shape makes it a natural for most sandwiches.

Spinach

The dark green leaves of spinach usually come with the stems attached. Widely available both loose and prewashed in plastic bags, it's a hearty green that's good both raw and cooked.

And for those who like to explore possibilities . . . these are other wonderful greens that are also widely available now:

Belgian Endive

Part of the chicory family, it is recognized by its tapered, tightly packed yellowish white leaves. A bit pricey, Belgian endive is primarily used in salads but is also good in prepared foods.

Chicory (Curly Endive)

A bitter green that is best combined with more delicate greens. Because of its curly, sprawling texture, it is often used as a salad accent and as a garnish.

Escarole

Its broad, bitter leaves are often used in soups and other cooked foods.

Napa

Once used only in Asian cooking, this firmly packed, elongated head of tender greens is best suited for stir-frying, adding to soups, and eating raw with vinaigrette dressings (see Asian Cabbage Salad, page 17). Used interchangeably with Chinese cabbage.

Radicchio

A small, deep red, head lettuce with a bitter bite that adds nice color to a salad. A bit more expensive than the others but, used as an accent, a little bit goes a long way.

Watercress

A tart, pepper-flavored, tender-leaf lettuce used for a salad accent or as a garnish.

Don't be surprised if you find greens in specialty stores, or even on your supermarket produce counters, that aren't listed here. Give them a try! The new varieties and cross breeds offer one more way to add an extra zing to your salad bowl.

Tips on Preparing Greens

- Wash your greens! I know, you've heard mixed views on this, but I say, without a doubt, that greens should be washed under cold running water and the discolored outer leaves discarded. Then they can be spun in a salad spinner or drained and patted dry with paper towels. Leafier varieties may be dunked in a tub of cold water (to remove any grit or sand) and then dried.
- You can clean greens ahead of time, but for best results, don't wash more than a day in advance. And for the freshest salad, cut or tear the greens as close as possible to the time you plan to eat them.
- Store greens in the vegetable compartment of the refrigerator.
- Instead of tearing or cutting greens into 1-inch pieces, why not wedge them, fan them, shred them, or even create cups from the leaves? These sure might raise a few eyebrows at your table . . . they do at mine.

About Bagged Salads . . .

Most of us have seen the selection of bagged greens beside all the loose greens at our produce counters. They're available in all sorts of combinations—one of my favorites is a precut salad mix containing iceberg and romaine, accented with spinach and a few other leafy greens. These cost a bit more, but there's no waste, and they sure are great time savers since all the washing and cutting have already been done. And with today's modern technology, they have an extended shelf life, which means they hold up well in the refrigerator. A few even come with dressings and croutons enclosed. What could be more convenient?!

Salad Toppers

If you want to "hearty up" your salad, try a combination of the following toppers. Each of them gives a green salad a nice accent, and may be served as is while some work well steamed, grilled, or even marinated.

Fresh Veggies   Tomatoes, onions, cucumbers, carrots, scallions, celery, bell peppers, radishes, green beans, alfalfa sprouts, avocado, broccoli, and more.

Fresh Fruit   Sliced oranges, melons, apples, fresh peaches and plums, grapes, strawberries, and more.

Canned or Frozen Veggies and Fruit   Usually thawed and/or drained. Cherries, mandarin oranges, mixed fruit salad, peas, corn, beans, mushrooms, olives, kidney beans, garbanzo beans (chick peas), beets, and more.

Cheese   Almost any variety shredded, sliced, diced, or crumbled and placed on top, or even added to, dressings. And, of course, don't forget cottage cheese, sour cream, and yogurt.

Cooked or Canned Meat, Poultry, or Fish   A great way to use leftovers, or you can get a selection of these fresh from the deli.

Others   Don't forget the crunchies and chewies! There are croutons, fried, crispy onions, nuts, sunflower seeds, raisins, and more possibilities. And, just as every special ice cream dish has a cherry on top, you can top a special salad with a sliced, hard-boiled egg to give it that really finished look.

Honey Mustard Dressing

about 2 cups

Put away those bottled dressings, 'cause this is one of the best dressings I've ever had. (I always make a double batch so I won't run out!)

1 ¼ cups mayonnaise
⅓ cup honey
⅔ cup vegetable oil
1 tablespoon white vinegar
1 teaspoon minced onion flakes
2 tablespoons minced fresh parsley
2 tablespoons prepared yellow mustard

In a medium-sized bowl, whisk together all the ingredients until smooth and creamy. Serve immediately or cover and chill until ready to use.

NOTE: This is great tossed with spinach or mixed salad greens, in seafood or chicken salads, and over grilled chicken or steak.

11

Red Wine Vinaigrette

1 ⅓ cups

Here's a dressing that will light up a salad with just the right touch.

½ cup olive oil
½ cup red wine vinegar
2 cloves garlic, minced
¼ cup finely chopped onions
¼ cup finely chopped fresh parsley
1 ½ teaspoons sugar
½ teaspoon salt
⅛ teaspoon pepper

In a small bowl, combine all the ingredients together and whisk well. Cover and chill overnight before serving.

NOTE: This is great not only on salads . . . try it as a marinade for chicken, fish, or veggies, too! It's got so many uses that it's a super addition to your dressing lineup.

Mandarin Spinach Salad

4 to 6 servings

You're seeing this recipe in more and more restaurants today—and there's a reason! Go ahead and find out . . .

> 1 package (10 ounces) cleaned fresh spinach
> 1 cup bottled Italian dressing
> ⅓ cup sugar
> 2 teaspoons poppy seed
> 1 can (11 ounces) mandarin oranges, drained
> ¼ cup toasted slivered almonds

Rinse the spinach leaves well in cold water and remove stems; dry well between layers of paper towels. In a large salad bowl, combine the Italian dressing, sugar, and poppy seed. Toss with the spinach, mandarin oranges, and almonds. Serve immediately.

NOTE: You can substitute peeled, fresh orange sections for the canned mandarin oranges. And try this dressing over fresh fruit salad.

Thousand Island Dressing

1 ½ cups

This recipe, which originated at a hotel in the Thousand Islands area of central New York State, is very similar to what most of us think of as Russian dressing. Although there are many variations of Russian and Thousand Island dressings, this one is the quickest.

> 1 cup mayonnaise
> ¼ cup ketchup
> ¼ cup sweet relish

In a small bowl, mix the mayonnaise and ketchup until thoroughly blended. Fold in the relish; serve immediately or cover and chill until ready to use.

NOTE: Use within 3 to 5 days and mix before each use. It's the perfect dressing because you always have the ingredients on hand.

Pineapple Honey Dressing

about ⅔ cup

Zesty and fruity, this dressing is what summer is all about.

> ½ cup fresh pineapple chunks
> 2 tablespoons fresh lemon or lime juice
> 2 tablespoons honey
> 1 tablespoon vegetable oil
> ¼ teaspoon salt
> ¼ teaspoon pepper

Purée all the ingredients in a food processor or blender. Serve immediately or cover and chill until ready to use.

NOTE: This is great served over spinach salad or grilled meat or chicken. And if you'd rather, you can use a drained 8-ounce can of pineapple chunks (or crushed pineapple or pineapple tidbits) instead of fresh pineapple.

Blue Cheese Dressing

about 2 cups

Attention blue cheese lovers—after you taste this one, you'll never buy bottled again! (And maybe you'll even convert some non–blue cheese lovers.)

 1½ cups sour cream
 ¼ cup mayonnaise
 1 tablespoon vegetable oil
 1 tablespoon white vinegar
 4 ounces blue cheese, broken up
 Dash of pepper
 Salt to taste (optional)

Place all the ingredients, except the salt, in a blender. Blend to desired consistency, then add salt, if needed. Serve immediately or cover and chill until ready to use.

NOTE: If you like your dressing chunky, add some crumbled blue cheese after blending.

Asian Cabbage Salad

2 cups

In the mood for something crunchy, full of flavor, and a real crowd-pleaser? With these great Asian tastes, we've made it our own all-American-easy.

> 2 tablespoons peanut oil
> ½ cup sesame seed
> 4 medium-sized cloves garlic, minced
> 2 tablespoons soy sauce
> ¼ cup white vinegar
> ½ cup sugar
> ¾ cup vegetable oil
> 1 head Napa or Chinese cabbage, washed and cut
>   into bite-sized pieces

In a medium-sized saucepan, warm the peanut oil over medium heat. Sauté the sesame seed and garlic for 3 to 5 minutes, until the seeds are golden brown. Reduce the heat to medium-low and add the soy sauce, vinegar, sugar, and vegetable oil; continue to cook for 2 more minutes. Place the cabbage in a large bowl and pour the desired amount of warm dressing over it, tossing to coat the cabbage evenly.

NOTE: Refrigerate any remaining dressing for up to 1 month. Just reheat before adding to more cabbage.

Warm Honey Walnut Dressing

1 ½ cups

Don't let the name scare you . . . Try it once and you'll forget about the old standbys. (Watch—it's sure to become a family favorite!)

> 2 tablespoons peanut oil
> ¼ cup chopped walnuts
> ⅓ cup honey
> ¼ cup maple syrup
> ½ cup bottled Italian dressing
> 2 heads Boston, Bibb, or romaine lettuce, cut into bite-sized pieces
> 1 can (17 ounces) sweet dark pitted cherries, drained

Place the oil and walnuts in a medium-sized saucepan and warm over medium heat until the nuts are slightly brown but not burned. Add the honey, maple syrup, and Italian dressing; reduce heat to low and simmer for 5 to 7 minutes, until hot. Place the lettuce in a large bowl and toss with the dressing. Top with the cherries.

NOTE: Serve this with your favorite pork or poultry dish for a combo that is indescribably good.

Farmer's Dressing

about 2 cups

*Talk about a light, creamy dressing . . . I got this from a farmer in the
Northeast during the cucumber harvest a few years back—and am I glad!*

> 1 medium-sized cucumber, cut into small chunks
> 1 cup sour cream
> 1 cup mayonnaise
> ½ teaspoon garlic powder
> ¼ teaspoon pepper

In a food processor or blender, blend all ingredients on medium-
high speed until smooth. Serve immediately or cover and chill until
ready to use.

*NOTE: No cucumbers? No problem! Just substitute a medium-sized zuc-
chini—the results are just as good.*

Back-to-Basics Vinaigrette

1¼ cups

Every dressing doesn't have to be totally different. Once in a while it's time to get "back to basics."

> 1 cup olive oil
> ¼ cup white vinegar
> 1 teaspoon garlic powder
> 1 teaspoon onion powder
> 1 teaspoon salt
> ½ teaspoon pepper

Place all the ingredients in a medium-sized bowl. Using a whisk, mix until well blended. Serve immediately or cover and chill until ready to use.

NOTE: If the olive oil in the dressing turns cloudy after chilling, let it stand at room temperature for a few minutes, then whisk again.

Creamy Caesar Dressing

about 2½ cups

Did you know that the original Caesar salad was invented at a restaurant in Tijuana, Mexico? And that anchovies were not an original ingredient? Here's my version of this now world-famous dressing.

> 1½ cups mayonnaise
> ¾ cup half-and-half or milk
> ¾ cup grated Parmesan cheese
> 2 cloves garlic
> ¼ teaspoon pepper
> 3 anchovy fillets *or* ⅛ teaspoon salt

Combine all the ingredients in a blender and blend on medium-high speed, scraping the sides occasionally, until smooth and creamy. Serve immediately or cover and chill until ready to use.

NOTE: Just before serving, toss gently with cut romaine lettuce and top with croutons **Do not toss with the greens until ready to serve.**

Japanese Ginger Dressing

1½ cups

If you've ever tasted the creamy salad dressing served in Japanese res-
taurants, you probably wondered, as I did, just what was in it. Well,
here's the answer! Now you can make it at home without any fuss . . .
And use chopsticks, of course, for an authentic experience.

>½ cup peanut oil
>¼ cup white vinegar
>¼ cup water
>2 tablespoons soy sauce
>2 teaspoons lemon juice
>2 tablespoons ketchup
>2 teaspoons ground ginger
>2 teaspoons sugar
>½ teaspoon salt
>½ teaspoon pepper
>½ cup chopped onions

Combine all ingredients in a blender or food processor and blend
until smooth. Serve immediately or cover and chill until ready
to use.

NOTE: Just before serving, toss with coarsely shredded iceberg lettuce
and diced tomatoes.

Potato Pleasers

Baked or mashed—those are the two ways that most people make potatoes. And sure, they're good. But since most of us are potato lovers (I sure am!), we should remind ourselves how versatile they are. You can dice them, grate them, bake them, fry them, toss them, mash them, and even "salad" them.

The subtle taste of potatoes is easily enhanced by almost any flavor. A little tarragon and we're in France. . . . Some chili powder and we're in Mexico. Of course, I love them with good old ketchup, too. That brings me to French fries—an all-the-time winner, which get teamed with everything from gravy to cheese and even mayonnaise!

In addition to their versatility, other nice things about potatoes are their year-round availability and the fact that they have no fat and little sodium . . . naturally! Potatoes are said to be the least expensive vegetable per pound—a real bargain with all the ways we can use them *and* considering all their nutritional value.

Which potatoes are right for your different needs? You should find a lot of help in my potato tips on the following pages. Now, of course, it's best to bake the bakers and boil the boilers, but don't worry about that because it's really okay to bake a boiling potato and boil a baking potato. As I said before, they're so versatile!

So the next time you're making dinner, go for the spuds. After you try a few of these potato recipes, you're gonna know why I call potatoes the "everything, any-way vegetable"!

Potato Pleasers

Basic Guide to Potatoes

There are four basic potato categories. Within each category there are many varieties—and with the constant advances in agricultural technology, the number of varieties keeps growing!

Russet

A firm potato with a rough, brown skin, usually 4 to 6 inches long and about 2 inches around. It has a drier consistency than other potatoes and yields a fluffier cooked product. Ideal for frying because it doesn't absorb oil easily, and also ideal for baking. Idaho is one of the most popular Russet varieties.

Long White

Firm textured with a light brown, thin skin. Ideal for boiling, mashing, or sautéing. The "almost everything" potato. White Rose is one of the most popular Long White varieties.

Round Red

Very firm, with a delicate red skin. Ideal for boiling or steaming, which means it's great for making potato salad! Skin can be left on for a nutritional as well as a color boost!

Round White

Light colored, with a waxlike finish. The all-purpose potato.

Specialty varieties are popping up more and more these days, and range from butter or yellow potatoes, with a rich, buttery consistency, to blue Carib, with a gray-blue skin, and rose fir, recognizable by its delicate, light pink skin. Young or new potatoes, also called creamers, are potatoes picked before reaching their full maturity. Available with red or light tan skin, they have a tender, moist, and creamy texture. (I guess that's how they got the name *creamers*.)

We don't want to forget about sweet potatoes. They're a tuber vegetable native to Central and South America. Although there are many varieties, we can easily recognize the most popular ones by their tapered shape and deep-orange skin. Even though most times sweet potatoes and yams can be used interchangeably, they are technically very different, since yams are a tropical root vegetable recognized by their lighter-colored skin. Yams are not as widely available as sweet potatoes in the United States, and the few that are available here are imported from the Caribbean.

About Convenience Potatoes . . .

No, they don't "grow that way," but there sure are a lot to "pick" from. I'm talking about frozen and canned potatoes. There are so many choices of potatoes in the supermarket freezer section. Why, they can be heated and ready to serve in no time, with no peeling, dicing, or scrubbing. We need that sometimes! And if we want, we can certainly jazz them up a bit before serving. Canned potatoes are great, too, 'cause they are always ready-to-go and available for us right in our pantries.

Choosing and Storing Potatoes

- Potatoes are often sorted by size. I recommend looking for medium-sized potatoes (size varies with each variety) that are free from bruises and cuts and have a firm skin.
- Avoid wrinkled potatoes, ones that have begun to sprout, and ones with green patches.
- Choose potatoes with uniform shapes and sizes; they will cook more evenly.
- No, fresh whole potatoes do not have to be stored in the refrigerator. Store them loose (not in plastic bags) in a bin or rack (to allow air to circulate around them) in a cool (45°F. to 50°F.) dark place that is well ventilated. Kept this way, they should last for several weeks.
- Do not store potatoes with onions or garlic, since they exchange mold-producing gases.
- Store peeled and cut potatoes in cold water in the refrigerator; they'll last this way for several days.
- To maintain freshness, cover or tightly wrap leftover potatoes and store in the refrigerator.

Tips for Terrific Baked Potatoes

- Always scrub potato skins well under cold, running water.
- Prick potatoes with a fork before baking to shorten the baking time.
- Here's another way to cut down on baking time: Insert a heated metal skewer through each potato and leave it in during baking. (Heating the skewer first "seals" the potato and prevents it from turning dark in the center.) Be careful when inserting and removing the hot skewers.

- Rub a bit of olive or vegetable oil on the outside of the potatoes before baking to make their skins crispy.
- Do *not* wrap potatoes in aluminum foil for baking. Foil holds in moisture and steams potatoes, resulting in a "boiled" taste and texture.
- Turn the potatoes over halfway through the baking time to prevent browning of the undersides where they touch the baking tray or oven rack.
- To "bake" potatoes in the microwave, wash but don't dry them. Pierce, then wrap them in microwave-safe paper towels and place 1 inch apart on a microwave rack. Cook according to your oven's guidelines, turning potatoes once during cooking. Don't exceed the recommended cooking time because potatoes will continue to cook after they're removed from the oven. **Be sure *not* to use metal skewers or aluminum foil in the microwave**.
- If baking more than 10 potatoes at a time, it's best to use the conventional oven method instead of the microwave.
- A baked potato is ready when a fork easily pierces its skin. If the potato is hard, bake it a little longer. However, be careful not to overbake, or the underskin will dry up.
- If potatoes baked to doneness are being held for over 10 minutes before serving, wrap them in foil. This will enhance the appearance of the skin by reducing shriveling.
- Instead of using a knife to open a baked potato (a knife flattens the surface and alters the normal fluffy texture of a baked spud), insert the tines of a fork in a straight line through the top of the potato, then press the ends toward the center to "pop" it open. Be careful—you may need to hold onto the potato with a napkin if it's too hot to handle.

Potato Toppers

Baked potatoes are great topped with leftover stews and cream-style soups. My other favorite toppings are

- sour cream
- shredded cheese
- gravy
- chili
- lightly cooked vegetables (even frozen and canned veggies are topping winners)

If you want to keep potatoes healthy, you'll find it's easy, since they're naturally low in fat and calories. You can keep them that way by offering low-fat toppings to go along with them, such as

- plain nonfat yogurt with chopped scallions
- low-fat cottage cheese and chives
- stewed tomatoes
- steamed broccoli florets or julienned carrots
- spicy mustard or salsa

As I always say, you know your own dos and don'ts, likes and dislikes, so do your own thing!

Bag 'n' Bake

4 to 6 servings

Here's a recipe that'll have the kids begging to help you. It's so easy and such fun . . . yummy, too!

> ¼ teaspoon salt
> ⅛ teaspoon pepper
> 1½ teaspoons paprika
> 1½ teaspoons onion powder
> 1½ teaspoons garlic powder
> ¼ cup vegetable oil
> 4 medium-sized potatoes, cut into ¼-inch slices

Preheat the oven to 350°F. In a plastic food storage bag, combine the salt, pepper, paprika, onion powder, and garlic powder. Place the oil in a shallow bowl and dip the potato slices in the oil. Then place the potato slices in the plastic bag, close tightly, and shake to completely coat the potatoes. Place the potato slices on a baking sheet that has been coated with nonstick vegetable spray. Bake for 35 to 40 minutes, or until golden and crispy.

NOTE: If you usually use white-skinned potatoes, try this with red-skinned potatoes for a change.

Potato Pockets

20 pockets

I bet they won't keep their hands in their pockets with these around! Maybe you should make an extra batch, 'cause they disappear like magic.

> 1 pound (about 2 to 3 large) potatoes, peeled, cubed, cooked, and drained
> 1 small onion, chopped
> 3 tablespoons butter or margarine
> ½ teaspoon salt
> ¼ teaspoon pepper
> 2 packages (10 ounces each) refrigerator buttermilk biscuits

Preheat the oven to 375°F. Place the potatoes in a large bowl; set aside. In a small skillet, sauté the onion in the butter until browned. Add the onion to the potatoes along with the salt and pepper. Mash by hand or with an electric beater; set aside. Separate each biscuit and flatten. Place a heaping tablespoon of the potato mixture into the center of each biscuit. Fold biscuit dough in half to form a half-circle, covering the potato mixture, and pinch the edges together with your fingers. Bake on a cookie sheet for 10 to 12 minutes, or until golden brown.

NOTE: If you want to jazz up the flavor a little, add ¼ teaspoon of garlic powder along with the other seasonings.

Spud Stuffing

4 to 6 servings

Can't decide on stuffing or mashed potatoes? Well, look no further 'cause now you can have both in one!

> 1½ pounds potatoes, peeled, cooked, and mashed (about 4 medium-sized potatoes or 4 cups mashed potatoes)
> 1 tablespoon butter
> 1 medium-sized onion, minced
> ½ cup sliced celery
> 1½ teaspoons salt
> ⅛ teaspoon pepper
> 2 teaspoons poultry seasoning
> 1 egg, beaten

Preheat the oven to 375°F. Place the mashed potatoes in a large bowl; set aside. Melt the butter in a medium-sized skillet over medium-high heat; add the onions and celery and sauté until tender but not brown. Add to the potatoes, along with the salt, pepper, and poultry seasoning. Add the egg and mix well. Place in a 7" × 11" glass baking dish that has been coated with nonstick vegetable spray and bake for 40 minutes, or until the sides and top are golden.

NOTE: Try this for the holidays and be a real kitchen hero.

Cheesy Herbed Mashed Potatoes

6 to 8 servings

Everybody loves mashed potatoes, but these have something special. Now instead of plain mashed potatoes, why not give your meal an easy cheesy bite?

3 pounds (about 4 large) baking potatoes, peeled and quartered
¼ cup (½ stick) butter or margarine
¾ cup sliced scallions (2 to 3 scallions)
1 tablespoon chopped fresh basil or 1 teaspoon dried
1 tablespoon chopped fresh chives or 1 teaspoon dried
1 tablespoon chopped fresh dill or 1 teaspoon dried dillweed
1 teaspoon salt (or to taste)
½ teaspoon pepper
1½ cups (6 ounces) shredded mild Cheddar cheese
½ cup milk

In a large pot of boiling salted water, cook the potatoes for 20 to 25 minutes, or until tender; drain in a colander. Place the butter and scallions in the pot and cook over medium heat for 1 minute. Reduce the heat to low and stir in the basil, chives, dill, salt, and pepper. Return the drained potatoes to the pot and add the cheese and milk. Remove from heat and mash with a potato masher or beat with an electric beater until smooth.

NOTE: If you like your potatoes a little less cheesy, don't be afraid to cut the amount of cheese to 1 cup. They'll still be packed with flavor.

Crispy Sweets

5 to 6 servings

Is your family getting bored with French fries? Well, here's a sweet way to surprise them.

> 1½ pounds (3 to 4) sweet potatoes
> ½ cup vegetable oil
> 2 tablespoons maple or pancake syrup
> ⅛ teaspoon ground nutmeg
> ⅛ teaspoon ground cinnamon

Wash the potatoes well. Cut each potato in half lengthwise, then cut each half lengthwise into 3 wedges. In a medium-sized skillet, heat the oil over medium-high heat. Place half of the potatoes in the hot oil, turning and cooking until they are crispy and brown. Remove the potatoes from the skillet and drain on paper towels. Place on a cookie sheet and keep warm in a 200°F. oven. Repeat with the remaining potatoes. In a shallow bowl, combine the syrup, nutmeg, and cinnamon. Using a pastry brush, brush the potato wedges with the syrup mixture; serve immediately.

NOTE: You may need to add an additional ¼ cup of oil for the second batch of potatoes.

Potato Pudding Squares

6 to 9 servings

My mom made this on special occasions . . . Now you can make any night special!

> 2 pounds (about 5 large) potatoes, cut into chunks
> 1 cup onion chunks (about 1 medium-sized onion)
> 2 eggs
> ⅔ cup vegetable oil
> 1½ teaspoons salt
> ½ teaspoon white pepper
> 1 tablespoon chopped fresh parsley
> ½ cup all-purpose flour

Preheat the oven to 350°F. Place all ingredients, except the flour, in a food processor. Process until just slightly coarse. Pour into a large bowl and mix in the flour. Pour into an 8-inch square glass baking dish that has been well coated with nonstick vegetable spray. Bake for 1 hour and 20 minutes, or until the top is golden brown.

NOTE: This works best if allowed to cool for about 20 minutes before cutting. It's also a great dish to make ahead of time and reheat.

Double Stuffers

6 servings

These might be a little extra work, but they're definitely worth the effort.

      6 medium-sized potatoes
      ½ teaspoon salt
      ¼ teaspoon pepper
      ¼ cup sour cream
      3 tablespoons butter or margarine
      ¼ teaspoon onion powder
      Paprika for sprinkling

Preheat the oven to 400°F. Scrub the potatoes and pierce the skins with a fork. Bake for 55 minutes, or until tender. Slice each potato lengthwise about 1 inch deep and scoop out the pulp; place in a medium-sized bowl. Add the salt, pepper, sour cream, butter, and onion powder and beat with an electric mixer. Spoon back into the potato shells and lightly sprinkle tops with paprika. Bake for 30 minutes, or until potatoes start to brown on top.

NOTE: These can be prepared and frozen for up to one month before baking, if wrapped well. Just thaw in the refrigerator overnight and bake as directed.

Swell Potatoes

5 to 6 servings

The batter will swell when these are fried . . . Your head will swell with all the compliments!

> 4 medium-sized potatoes
> 1¼ cups all-purpose flour
> ½ teaspoon salt
> ½ teaspoon onion powder
> ½ teaspoon garlic powder
> ½ teaspoon dried dillweed
> ½ teaspoon mustard powder
> ½ teaspoon cayenne pepper
> 1 cup milk
> 1 egg
> ½ inch vegetable oil for frying
> Salt for sprinkling (optional)

Wash the potatoes and cut into ¼-inch thick slices. In a large bowl, combine the flour, salt, onion powder, garlic powder, dillweed, mustard powder, and cayenne pepper. In a small bowl, beat the milk and egg, then add to the flour mixture to form a smooth batter. In a large skillet or a deep fryer, heat the oil over medium-high heat. Dip the potato slices in the batter, then fry them until crisp and brown. Drain on paper towels and sprinkle with salt, if desired.

NOTE: Since these swell, they're best when served immediately.

Sweet Potato Volcanoes

6 servings

With each bite you'll experience an explosion of Hawaiian goodness.

6 medium-sized sweet potatoes
½ cup orange juice
3 tablespoons butter
1 teaspoon salt
1 can (8 ounces) crushed pineapple, drained
½ cup chopped pecans (optional)

Preheat the oven to 375°F. Scrub the potatoes and pierce the skins with a fork. Bake the potatoes for 1 hour, or until tender. Cut a 1-inch lengthwise strip from the top of each potato. Carefully scoop the pulp from the potato shell and place in a large bowl. Beat in the orange juice, butter, and salt until fluffy. Stir in the pineapple, then use the mixture to stuff the potato shells. Sprinkle with pecans, if desired. Bake for 15 to 20 minutes, or until completely warmed through.

NOTE: These are just the thing if you're looking for dishes to prepare the day before serving. Just cover and refrigerate them, then bake as directed right before dinner—but you may have to bake them for an additional 10 minutes, since the filling will be cold.

Potato Pleasers

Golden Potato Nuggets

8 servings

With their Tex-Mex flavor, these nuggets are worth their weight in gold—
a sure treasure with any meal.

1½ cups dry bread crumbs
1 teaspoon onion powder
1 teaspoon chili powder
1 teaspoon salt
½ teaspoon pepper
3 pounds (about 8 medium-sized) potatoes, cut into
    quarters
½ cup (1 stick) butter, melted

Preheat the oven to 350°F. In a medium-sized bowl, combine the
bread crumbs, onion powder, chili powder, salt, and pepper. Dip
the potato quarters into the butter, then roll in the crumb mixture.
Place on a greased cookie sheet and bake for 60 minutes, or until
light brown and fork tender.

NOTE: These are best right from the oven . . . Mmm!

"OOH" Gratin Potatoes

4 to 6 servings

Here's one of my family favorites that'll have your family saying "OOH Gratin . . . OOH it's so GOOD!!" ™

> ½ cup milk
> 1 teaspoon Italian seasoning
> ½ teaspoon salt
> 1 teaspoon onion powder
> ¼ teaspoon white pepper
> 3 medium-sized potatoes, peeled and cut into ¼-inch
>   slices
> 2 tablespoons butter or margarine
> ½ cup (2 ounces) shredded Cheddar cheese
> 2 tablespoons grated Parmesan cheese
> Paprika for sprinkling

Preheat the oven to 350°F. In a small bowl, combine the milk, Italian seasoning, salt, onion powder, and pepper. Arrange the potato slices in a greased 2-quart casserole dish. Pour the milk mixture over the potatoes and dot with the butter. Cover and bake for 1 hour, or until the potatoes are tender. Remove the cover and sprinkle the cheeses and paprika over the potatoes. Bake, uncovered, for 8 to 10 minutes more, until the cheeses are melted. Serve hot.

NOTE: If you feel like going a little heavier on the seasonings, go ahead! It'll make it fuller tasting. In fact, I like it better that way.

Potato Pleasers

Sweet Potato Puff

4 to 6 servings

Take your table a step up from everyday with this sweet potato treat from North Carolina.

3 cups cooked and mashed sweet potatoes (about 4
    medium-sized potatoes)
3 tablespoons butter
¾ cup milk
Dash of pepper
2 eggs, separated
¼ teaspoon salt

Preheat the oven to 375°F. In a large bowl, with an electric beater, whip the cooked potatoes with the butter, milk, and pepper. Beat in the egg yolks. In a small bowl, with an electric beater, whip the egg whites with the salt until stiff; fold into the potato mixture. Place in a greased 1½-quart casserole dish and bake for 30 minutes, or until top is lightly browned.

NOTE: This is best served right from the oven.

Cheddar Potato Patties

about 36 patties

Melted Cheddar cheese and mashed potatoes . . . two of my favorites in one great side dish.

8 medium-sized potatoes, peeled, cut into quarters, and boiled until tender, drained (Do not allow to cool.)
⅓ cup milk
4 tablespoons butter or margarine
2 tablespoons chopped fresh parsley
1½ teaspoons salt
¼ teaspoon white pepper
½ teaspoon onion powder
¾ cup (3 ounces) shredded Cheddar cheese
2 eggs
1¼ cups dry bread crumbs

In a large bowl, combine the hot, cooked potatoes, milk, and butter. With an electric beater, whip until smooth. Add the parsley, salt, pepper, onion powder, and cheese. Mix well and let cool slightly. Preheat the broiler. Shape the potato mixture into 1½-inch balls. Place the eggs in a shallow dish and beat; place the bread crumbs in another shallow dish. Dip the potato balls into the eggs, then into the bread crumbs. Place on a cookie sheet that has been well coated with nonstick vegetable spray. Flatten slightly with your palm. Broil each side for 4 to 6 minutes, or until golden brown.

NOTE: What a great way to use leftover mashed potatoes! But if they're already seasoned, be sure to cut down on the salt and pepper when making these.

Simple Potato Soufflé

6 to 8 servings

The French might call this a soufflé, but I call it OOH-la-la GOOD!!

> 4 cups hot instant mashed potatoes or 3 pounds
>   potatoes, peeled, cooked, and mashed
> 1 package (8 ounces) cream cheese, softened
> 1 scallion, finely chopped (about ⅓ cup)
> ¼ cup chopped pimiento
> 1 egg, beaten
> 1 teaspoon salt
> ⅛ teaspoon pepper
> ½ teaspoon mustard powder

Preheat the oven to 350°F. In a large bowl, mix the mashed potatoes and cream cheese with an electric beater until well blended. Add the remaining ingredients and mix well. Spoon into a 1½-quart casserole dish that has been coated with nonstick vegetable spray. Bake for 40 to 45 minutes, or until brown around the edges.

NOTE: Serve this right from the oven to get that puffy, soufflé-like texture.

Your Own Potato Skins

12 potato halves

No need to dine out to enjoy these ... You can make them so easily right at home!

>   6 baking potatoes
>   ½ cup vegetable oil
>   1 teaspoon salt
>   1 teaspoon onion powder
>   1½ teaspoons chili powder

Preheat the oven to 400°F. Scrub the potatoes and pierce the skins with a fork. Microwave for 12 to 15 minutes or bake for 45 to 60 minutes, until fork-tender. Let potatoes cool slightly, then cut each potato in half lengthwise and hollow out each half with a spoon, leaving some potato around the edges. Save the potato pulp for another use. In a medium-sized bowl, combine the remaining ingredients. Rub the potato skins, inside and out, with the oil mixture and place on a 9″ × 13″ cookie sheet. Bake for 40 to 45 minutes, or until the edges are crispy and brown.

NOTE: The potato skin is only the beginning! Top these with your favorite fillings ... Try chili, sour cream, applesauce, melted cheese, or even chicken à la king. The possibilities are endless. And don't forget—true potato-skin lovers even eat them plain.

Autumn Sweet Potatoes

6 to 8 servings

Don't wait till autumn to make this, 'cause you'll miss out on year-round "oohs"s and "ahh"s.

> 1 can (40 ounces) sweet potatoes or yams, drained
> and cut into chunks
> 1 can (20 ounces) pineapple chunks
> 1 cup pitted prunes
> 1 can (16 ounces) sliced carrots, drained
> ¼ cup maple or pancake syrup
> ¼ cup firmly packed light brown sugar

Preheat the oven to 350°F. Place the sweet potatoes in a large bowl. Drain the pineapple, reserving ½ cup liquid; combine the drained pineapple, prunes, and carrots with the potatoes. Add the maple syrup and brown sugar to the reserved pineapple liquid; mix until blended, then pour over the sweet potato mixture. Transfer to a 2-quart casserole dish that has been coated with nonstick vegetable spray. Cover and bake for 40 minutes, or until hot and bubbly.

NOTE: This tastes better when served the second day, so be sure to bake a double batch.

Oven-Roasted Potatoes

6 to 8 servings

Sometimes there's nothing better than an "oldie but goodie." And this one sure hits the mark every time!

> 1 cup vegetable oil
> ½ teaspoon pepper
> 2 teaspoons salt
> 2 teaspoons paprika
> 1 teaspoon garlic powder
> 1 teaspoon onion powder
> 2½ pounds (about 6 to 7) red-skinned potatoes,
>   washed and cut into 1-inch chunks

Preheat the oven to 400°F. In a large bowl, combine all the ingredients except the potatoes. Toss the potatoes in the mixture, coating evenly. Place on a cookie sheet and bake for 50 to 60 minutes, until crisp and golden brown.

NOTE: I serve these with dinner and also with breakfast as home fries.

True-Blue Potato Salad

about 6 servings

I've always been a blue cheese lover, but even if you aren't, you'll be surprised at what a great combination this is. Make a few batches for your next picnic or family get-together and watch this blue cheese winner make them green with envy.

> 1½ to 2 pounds (2 to 3 large) potatoes, cooked and
>   cut into ¾-inch cubes to yield 4 cups
> 1 cup diced celery
> ½ cup sliced scallions (about 4 scallions)
> 1¼ cups sour cream
> 2 tablespoons minced fresh parsley
> 2 tablespoons white wine vinegar
> ½ teaspoon celery seed
> ½ teaspoon salt
> ¼ teaspoon pepper
> ¾ cup (3 ounces) crumbled blue cheese

In a large bowl, combine the potato cubes, celery, and scallions; set aside. In a medium-sized bowl, combine the sour cream, parsley, vinegar, celery seed, salt, and pepper; mix well. Stir in the blue cheese. Pour over the potato mixture and toss lightly. Chill and serve.

Potatoes O'Brien

4 to 6 servings

I use frozen diced potatoes in this one and no one ever knows. The taste is so homemade (without all the work)!

> 6 tablespoons butter or margarine, divided
> 1 medium-sized onion, diced (about 1 cup)
> 1 large bell pepper, diced (about 1 cup)
> 1 teaspoon salt
> ¼ teaspoon black pepper
> 1 bag (32 ounces) frozen diced potatoes
> Paprika for sprinkling

Preheat the oven to 375°F. Melt 2 tablespoons butter in a medium-sized skillet over medium-high heat. Sauté the onions and bell pepper for 8 to 10 minutes, or until wilted. Melt the remaining butter and place in a large bowl. Mix in the salt and black pepper, add the potatoes, and toss. Add the onions and bell pepper and stir until thoroughly mixed. Pour into a 9" × 13" glass baking dish that has been coated with nonstick vegetable spray and sprinkle the top with paprika. Bake, covered, for 15 minutes. Uncover and bake for 15 more minutes.

NOTE: This is best when served immediately, but you can refrigerate any leftovers and still enjoy them a second time!

Creamy Peppery Potatoes

4 to 5 servings

I know, I know, the recipe says it serves 4 to 5 . . . but these are so good I could almost eat a whole batch myself.

> 2 pounds (4 to 5 large) potatoes, peeled and cut into
> large chunks
> ¼ cup bottled peppercorn ranch dressing or bottled
> pepper Parmesan dressing
> 2 tablespoons butter or margarine
> ½ teaspoon salt
> ⅛ teaspoon pepper

Place the potatoes in a large pot, add enough water to cover, and bring to a boil. Cook the potatoes for about 20 minutes, or until tender but firm. Drain the potatoes well, return them to the pot, and add the remaining ingredients. Mash or beat with an electric beater until mostly smooth and creamy, leaving just a few lumps for that homemade touch.

NOTE: If you're not going to serve these immediately, then make as directed and place the finished potatoes in a 1½-quart casserole dish that has been coated with nonstick vegetable spray, cover, and refrigerate until just before serving. Then bake in a preheated 350°F. oven for 20 minutes, or until hot.

Potato Pleasers

Salt City Potatoes

6 servings

"Salt City" (Syracuse, New York) is like my second home, so when I make these it's like coming home to an old friend. I bet you'll agree!

> 3 pounds small new potatoes
> 4 quarts water
> 1 cup salt
> ½ cup (1 stick) butter

Place the potatoes and water in a large pot. Pour the salt over the potatoes, cover, and bring to a boil. Reduce heat to medium and cook for 25 minutes, or until the potatoes are fork-tender. Melt the butter and place in a large bowl. Dip the hot potatoes in the melted butter and serve.

NOTE: For that authentic Central New York flavor, use an additional ½ cup of salt. And if you have any of these left over, they're perfect for making home fries.

Rice to Entice

Do you have any rice horror stories? It's okay, 'cause at one time or another most of us have made rice that was so sticky we could have used it to hang wallpaper, or maybe it was so hard and crunchy you couldn't chew it.

If these stories sound familiar, I hope you haven't let those few bad experiences steer you away from making rice for good. Come back to a new way with rice. It's an energy food that's quick—a grain that can be added to almost everything from soup to dessert, and has no fat, cholesterol, or sodium.

Most of the rice eaten in the United States is long-grain white rice. It's the best choice for salads and prepared rice dishes because the finished rice grains are dry, light, and fluffy, and they tend to separate. Short-grain rice cooks up moister and stickier, and that's the type usually served in Asian restaurants. (Do you think that's because it's easier to pick up with chopsticks?) Instant and quick-cooking types of rice are often "enriched" because nutrients are lost when rice companies process and parboil rice (which they do so that the rice cooks faster when we cook it). Enriching it puts back some of those lost nutrients.

Whether instant, long- or short-grain, brown, or enriched, rice really is easy to add to the side of our plates. It can be made on the stove top or in the oven. (My feeling about cooking rice in the microwave: Don't bother. It's really no quicker than the conventional methods. But microwaves *are* great for reheating it!) However you choose to make it, the tips and great recipes I've got on the following pages should really help you make winning rice every time.

It's time for a change, so why not entice with rice?!

Rice to Entice

Cooking Rice—The Basics

Although there are probably as many different ways to cook rice as there are types of rice, I've simplified it here. But if you have a secret formula that works for you, then don't stop doing it that way. . . . Do what works for you.

For instant and quick-cooking rice: Read the package. Instructions vary from brand to brand, and following the specific directions is the best way to ensure that the rice will come out right every time.

For all other popular types of rice (those typically found in the supermarket): Use 1 cup rice to between 2 and 2¼ cups water. Add 1 teaspoon salt to every 2 cups of water, and if you want, add 1 tablespoon of butter when making plain rice that's not going to be added to a special recipe. (I like that rich, buttery taste.)

If you prefer softer, stickier rice, add a bit more water and simmer it for a few extra minutes. If you prefer drier, fluffier rice, use a lower proportion of water to rice. **Remember: These are approximate amounts.** All rice packages should have directions, so follow those and see for yourself what works best with each particular brand.

Stove-Top Method In a medium-sized saucepan (or a stockpot for larger quantities), bring salted water to a boil over high heat. When boiling, stir in the rice. Reduce the heat to low, and cover the pot. Cook until the rice is tender—20 to 25 minutes for white rice and 35 to 45 minutes for wild or brown rice. **Unless you think the rice is scorching (which it shouldn't!), do not remove the cover or stir the rice while it is cooking.** When tender, remove the cover (be careful of the steam from inside the pan), and fluff the rice with a fork. There should be virtually no water left in the pan.

Oven Method Preheat the oven to 400°F. Place the rice, boiling water, and salt in a medium-sized casserole dish. Cover tightly and bake white rice for 20 to 25 minutes and brown or wild rice for 35 to 45 minutes. Uncover (be careful of the steam from inside the dish) and fluff the rice with a fork. There should be virtually no water left in the dish.

Instant and Precooked Rice Follow the package directions carefully. Instructions vary from brand to brand and, again, following the specific package directions is the best way to ensure that the rice will come out right!

Rice Tips

- Store uncooked rice in an airtight container in a cool, dry place. Stored properly, uncooked rice can last for a very long time. (I like to keep it in a clear container so I can easily see how much I've got on hand.)
- During cooking, rice swells to about four times its uncooked size, so be sure to use a big enough saucepan or casserole dish. (Otherwise, you could have a real mess on your hands!)
- While rice is cooking, don't lift the lid! Steam will escape, and steam is what cooks the rice.
- Except for the Basmati variety (which should be washed well, soaked, and picked through to remove small stones before cooking the same way as white rice), most rice shouldn't need to be washed before cooking. It retains more of its natural nutrients if it's unwashed.
- Cook your rice in chicken or beef broth instead of water to give it an extra flavor burst.
- Don't overstir it. Too much stirring breaks up rice and makes it mushy. Just stir it into the water, then let it cook. When it's done, fluff it with a fork.

Rice to Entice

- If you have plain (cooked in water and unseasoned) rice left over, you can stir it into prepared or instant vanilla pudding and top it with a sprinkle of ground cinnamon for a quick taste of rice pudding.
- Leftover rice is perfect for adding to any soup or stew.
- Leftover rice can be frozen in an airtight container and kept for up to a month or so.
- The microwave is great for reheating leftover rice. Just place the rice in a microwave-safe container, cover, and cook until just heated through. Cooking time varies with the power of your microwave.
- To reheat rice on the stove top, add about 2 tablespoons of water per cup of rice; cover, and warm for 4 to 5 minutes over medium heat, or just until heated through.

Lone Star Rice

6 servings

Looking for a change of pace? Try this for that perfect accompaniment to fried chicken or steak.

> 2 tablespoons vegetable oil
> 1 cup long-grain or whole-grain rice, uncooked
> 2 cloves garlic, minced
> 2½ cups ready-to-use beef broth (not condensed)
> 1 teaspoon ground cumin
> ½ teaspoon dried oregano
> 1 can (16 ounces) kidney beans, rinsed and drained
> ⅓ cup mild picante sauce
> ¼ cup sliced scallions (1 scallion)

In a large saucepan, heat the oil over medium heat and sauté the rice and garlic until the rice is slightly browned. Add the broth, cumin, and oregano and bring to a boil. Reduce heat, cover, and simmer for 20 minutes. Stir in the beans and remove from the heat. Let stand, covered, until the liquid is absorbed, about 5 minutes. Stir in the picante sauce and scallions.

NOTE: If you prefer, instead of the kidney beans you can use pinto or black beans, or even black-eyed peas.

Garlic Skillet Rice

5 cups

They'll never guess what the secret ingredient is . . . So let's keep it our secret.

3⅓ cups water
1½ cups long-grain or whole-grain rice, uncooked
2 tablespoons vegetable oil
½ cup angle-cut scallions (2 scallions)
2 cloves garlic, minced
1 large, firm tomato, cut into ½-inch cubes
   (about 1½ cups)
1 teaspoon salt
½ teaspoon dried dillweed
¼ cup bottled ranch dressing

In a large saucepan, bring the water to a boil. Add the rice, then reduce the heat and simmer for 20 minutes or until all the water is absorbed; set aside. In a large skillet, heat the oil over medium-high heat and sauté the scallions and garlic for 2 to 3 minutes. Add the tomato and continue to sauté for 2 to 3 more minutes. Add the cooked rice, salt, and dillweed and mix well. Add the ranch dressing and mix until heated through. Serve immediately.

NOTE: If you want this a bit more creamy, add an additional ¼ cup of ranch dressing . . . you know, the secret ingredient. (Ssh!) And you can try any of the ranch dressing flavors, like Caesar ranch, peppercorn ranch, or the others—they'll all work.

57

Rice and Broccoli Melt

6 to 8 servings

Here's a yummy way to have your rice and veggies all in one dish. (Wait till you see how thick and chunky it is!)

> 1 package (16 ounces) frozen broccoli, thawed and drained
> 3 tablespoons chopped scallions (about 1 scallion)
> 1 clove garlic, minced
> 1 tablespoon vegetable oil
> 2 cups hot cooked rice
> ⅓ cup mayonnaise
> 2 tablespoons soy sauce
> ½ cup (2 ounces) shredded Cheddar cheese
> ¾ cup French-fried onions, or bread crumbs
> (optional)

Preheat the oven to 350°F. Place the broccoli in a medium-sized bowl and add the scallions, garlic, oil, rice, mayonnaise, and soy sauce, mixing well. Put the mixture into a 1½-quart casserole dish that has been coated with nonstick vegetable spray and top with the cheese. Sprinkle with the French-fried onions, if desired. Cover and bake for 25 minutes, until the cheese has melted.

NOTE: Three-quarters of a cup of uncooked rice will make 2 cups of cooked rice.

It's so easy to make this recipe your own because you can use onions instead of scallions, fresh broccoli instead of frozen (just steam or boil it before adding), light mayonnaise instead of regular, and you can even add some pepperoni slices or other cooked sausage to make it a lunch or light supper dish all by itself!

Southwestern Layered Rice

4 to 6 servings

Do you have Taco Night at your house? Well, next time you do, try adding this to the menu. (It's a great side dish for any of your Mexican-style meals . . . and with fish, too!)

2 cups sour cream
2 teaspoons salt
¼ teaspoon pepper
1 tablespoon sugar
1 cup chopped scallions (about 3 scallions)
½ cup bacon bits
3 cups (12 ounces) shredded Cheddar cheese
3 cups cooked rice, divided

Preheat the oven to 425°F. In a medium-sized bowl, blend the sour cream, salt, pepper, and sugar by hand. In a large bowl, combine the scallions, bacon bits, and cheese. Place one third of the rice on the bottom of a 2-quart casserole dish that has been coated with nonstick vegetable spray. Layer one third of the sour cream mixture over the rice, then one third of the cheese. Repeat the layers, ending with a layer of cheese mixture on top. Bake for 30 minutes, or until bubbly and brown around the edges.

NOTE: You may substitute crispy, crumbled bacon for the bacon bits, if desired.

Winter Rice

4 to 6 servings

I first tried this dish on a cold, snowy night many winters ago, and it has since become a year-round family favorite (but the name stuck).

> 2 tablespoons butter or margarine
> 2 cups chopped onions (about 1 large onion)
> 1 cup long-grain or whole-grain rice, uncooked
> 2 cups ready-to-use (not condensed) chicken broth
> ¼ cup mayonnaise
> ½ cup grated Parmesan cheese
> ¼ teaspoon white pepper

Melt the butter in a large saucepan; sauté the onions over medium heat until they become slightly translucent, about 5 minutes. Add the rice and continue to sauté for 7 to 10 minutes, until the rice begins to brown. Add the remaining ingredients and reduce the heat to low; cover and simmer for 25 minutes, or until most of the liquid is absorbed. Turn off the heat and let the pan sit on the burner for 10 to 15 minutes more.

NOTE: This looks really fancy when garnished with scallion rings.

Rice to Entice

Rice Pie

6 to 8 servings

Everyone always wants "a piece of the pie"—well, everybody can have a cut of this one . . . and boy, will Mom approve!

2 tablespoons butter or margarine
1 can (4 ounces) sliced mushrooms or mushroom
    stems and pieces, drained
½ cup chopped onions
1 package (10 ounces) frozen chopped spinach,
    thawed and drained
1½ cups cooked instant rice
½ pint (8 ounces) heavy cream
2 eggs
1 teaspoon salt
¼ teaspoon white pepper
¼ teaspoon ground nutmeg, plus extra for sprinkling

Preheat the oven to 350°F. Melt the butter in a large skillet over medium-high heat, and sauté the mushrooms and onions until soft. Set aside. In a large bowl, combine the remaining ingredients, except the extra nutmeg. Add the mushrooms and onions, mixing well. Pour the mixture into a 9″ or 10″ pie plate that has been coated with nonstick vegetable spray. Sprinkle the top with extra nutmeg, if desired, and bake for 40 minutes, or until the center is set.

NOTE: Don't have any mushrooms? Don't worry—try this with sautéed bell pepper, asparagus, or broccoli pieces.

Rice to Entice

Maui Maui Rice

4 servings

Experience a Polynesian luau with every bite. All you need now is a grass skirt and some Hawaiian dancers!

>1⅓ cups water
>1 can (8 ounces) pineapple tidbits, undrained
>¼ cup firmly packed brown sugar
>¼ teaspoon ground cinnamon
>2 tablespoons soy sauce
>2 tablespoons butter
>½ cup chopped green bell pepper (about 1 large
>   pepper)
>1⅓ cups instant rice, uncooked
>10 maraschino cherries

In a medium-sized saucepan, combine all the ingredients except the rice and the maraschino cherries. Bring to a boil, then stir in the rice. Reduce the heat to low, cover, and simmer for 10 minutes, or until the liquid is absorbed. Garnish with the cherries.

NOTE: I recommend serving this with roast pork or turkey.

Spaghetti Rice

5 to 6 servings

Can't decide if the gang would rather have pasta or rice with dinner tonight? Don't worry . . . now they can have both!

4 tablespoons vegetable oil, divided
1 can (4 ounces) mushroom slices or mushroom
stems and pieces, drained
1 cup chopped onions (about 1 medium-sized onion)
1 cup (about 4 ounces) spaghetti, broken into 3-inch
pieces
1½ cups long-grain or whole-grain rice, uncooked
2 cans (13¾ ounces each) chicken broth
¼ teaspoon salt
⅛ teaspoon pepper

Heat 3 tablespoons oil in a large saucepan over medium-high heat; add the mushrooms and onions and sauté until lightly browned. Remove from the pan and set aside. Heat the remaining oil in the saucepan and brown the spaghetti over medium-low heat. (**Be careful—it browns quickly.**) Remove the pan from the heat and put the mushrooms and onions back into the pan. Add the remaining ingredients, mixing well. Bring the mixture to a boil, reduce the heat to low, cover, and cook for 20 minutes more, or until all the liquid is absorbed.

NOTE: If you're looking for a good make-ahead dish, this one freezes well.

63

Confetti Rice Salad

6 to 8 servings

Here's a side dish that will add so much color and fun to any picnic or barbecue plate.

2 cans (15 ounces each) black beans, rinsed and
    drained
2 cups cold cooked rice
1 cup chopped tomato (1 to 2 tomatoes)
¼ cup sliced scallions
¼ cup chopped fresh parsley
¼ cup olive oil
1 tablespoon cider vinegar
⅛ teaspoon hot pepper sauce
2 cloves garlic, minced
1 teaspoon salt
⅛ teaspoon pepper

In a large bowl, combine the beans and rice, mixing well. In a medium-sized bowl, combine the remaining ingredients, mixing well. Fold the tomato mixture into the bean mixture and refrigerate for at least 1 hour before serving.

"Lotsa" Pasta

Pasta, macaroni, noodles . . . they're everywhere! Pasta is a staple in Italian dishes, and a big part of Asian cooking, too. And what would our good old American macaroni and cheese be without pasta?

Pasta is incredibly popular as a main dish, but it sure makes a great side dish, too. It's quick, economical, and good for us. And we have so many choices! Most of us are familiar with dried pasta (which can be stored in the package it comes in or in an airtight container for quite a long time). But there are also lots of filled pastas and fresh, refrigerated pastas available, too. (Fresh pasta is perishable, so it will keep for three to four days in the refrigerator, and may be frozen for up to a month. And, no, frozen pasta does not have to be thawed before cooking.)

What about those colored pastas? Made with everything from beets to spinach, tomatoes, carrots, eggs, and herbs added right into the dough, colored pasta can really liven up a plate! Why not explore those as well as a few of my favorite pasta side dishes, including peanuty Thai Noodles (page 72), mouth-watering Garlic Tortellini (page 76), and garden-fresh-tasting Angelic Pasta (page 79) to see just how full-flavored a pasta side dish can be?

After you do, every time you need a dinner plate "pickup," you'll just pull out the pasta and have fun!

"Lotsa" Pasta

Cooking Pasta

- Generally, cook pasta in a large pot of boiling salted water, allowing about 1 quart of water for every ¼ pound of pasta. Slip pasta into the boiling water, a little at a time, so that the water keeps boiling. Stir immediately so the pasta doesn't stick together! Then stir pasta occasionally while it cooks, checking for doneness (see below), and drain.
- Fresh pasta cooks quickly, usually in 2 to 3 minutes; dried pasta takes between 7 and 12 minutes. Always check the package directions.
- To avoid having the pasta become soft and gluey, time your sauce so that it is ready as the pasta finishes cooking. If using the pasta in a cold salad, drain it, rinse it in cold water, then drain it again.
- Cooked pasta (without sauce) can last in the fridge for 3 to 4 days if lightly oiled before storing. To reheat, simply drop it into boiling water just long enough to heat through. Drain and use as you would after the first cooking.

Pasta Doneness

- Though pasta can be cooked to whatever point you want, most every pasta aficionado claims that pasta should be cooked "al dente," which literally means "to the tooth." To determine if pasta is done: Test it by cutting a piece with a fork or taking a bite. When the pasta has only a slight bit of uncooked core, it is al dente.
- When pasta is al dente, it gives you something to chew. I like it that way, but many people like their pasta soft. That's fine, too. Whatever makes us happy!
- When you cook pasta too long, it absorbs the maximum amount of cooking liquid. As a result, when sauce is added, the

"Lotsa" Pasta

dish can become weepy or watery. Pasta that is still a little firm is more likely to absorb some of the liquid from the sauce, thus preventing a soggy finished dish. And if you're planning to cook the pasta further, such as in a dish of baked lasagna, make sure the pasta is even firmer still.

Pasta Sauce Partners

Of course you can choose any pasta sauce to go with any pasta, but these work best:

PASTA TYPE	SAUCE
SHORT PASTA	HEAVY SAUCE
WIDE PASTA	HEAVY SAUCE
PASTA STRANDS	LIGHT SAUCE
PASTA WITH HOLES OR CREVICES	CHUNKY SAUCE
PASTA WITH RIDGES	WILL HOLD ANY SAUCE

Curly Cheddar Bake

8 servings

Everybody loves macaroni and cheese . . . but here's one with a difference!

1 pound rotini pasta
4 cups (16 ounces) shredded sharp Cheddar cheese,
    divided
½ cup (1 stick) butter or margarine
½ cup grated Parmesan cheese
6 eggs
2 cans (13 ounces each) evaporated milk
½ teaspoon mustard powder
1 teaspoon salt
½ teaspoon pepper

Preheat the oven to 350°F. Cook the rotini according to package directions; drain well and place in a large bowl. Add 3½ cups of the Cheddar cheese and stir until the cheese is melted. Add the butter, Parmesan cheese, and eggs; mix well. Add the remaining ingredients, except for the remaining Cheddar cheese. (The mixture will be fairly liquidy.) Pour into a 9" × 13" baking dish that has been coated with nonstick vegetable spray. Sprinkle with the remaining ½ cup Cheddar cheese and bake for 40 to 45 minutes, until the center is set.

NOTE: This is just as good the day after it's made!

Noodles, Peas, 'n' Cheese

6 to 8 servings

This'll help you put dinner together with no fuss because, after you've got your main dish set, you just have to mix your veggies and noodles together for this all-in-one side dish!

1 package (12 ounces) wide egg noodles
¼ cup (½ stick) butter or margarine, melted
1 can (10¾ ounces) Cheddar cheese soup
¾ cup sour cream
⅔ cup milk
1 teaspoon onion powder
½ teaspoon garlic powder
½ teaspoon salt
½ teaspoon white pepper
1 package (10 ounces) frozen peas

Preheat the oven to 350°F. Cook the noodles according to package directions and drain; place in a large bowl and mix with the melted butter. In a small bowl, combine the remaining ingredients, except the peas, until well blended. Add to the noodles and stir to evenly coat the noodles. Mix in the peas, then pour the mixture into a 2-quart casserole dish that has been coated with nonstick vegetable spray. Bake for 40 minutes, or until the top is light golden and crunchy.

Mushroom Charlotte

8 to 10 servings

Oh, no! Company's coming and you don't know what to serve! Well, this is so easy (and it'll taste like you worked on it all day).

> 1 pound orzo pasta, cooked and drained
> ¼ cup (½ stick) butter or margarine, melted
> 1 can (4 ounces) sliced mushrooms or mushroom stems and pieces, drained
> 1 envelope (from a 2-ounce box) onion soup mix

Preheat the oven to 350°F. Place the pasta in a large bowl; stir in the melted butter. Add the mushrooms and the onion soup mix; mix well. Place in a 1½-quart casserole dish and bake for 30 minutes, or until hot and bubbly. Serve immediately.

NOTE: This reheats well, so don't worry if you have leftovers!

Thai Noodles

6 to 8 servings

Here's an exotic pasta creation that'll make everybody want to come to your house for dinner.

1 pound linguine or spaghetti
1 cup creamy peanut butter
1 tablespoon finely chopped garlic
½ cup vegetable oil
2 tablespoons soy sauce
½ teaspoon crushed red pepper

Cook the pasta according to package directions. Meanwhile, in a medium-sized bowl, combine the remaining ingredients. Drain the pasta and place in a large bowl. Toss the peanut sauce with the hot cooked pasta and serve immediately.

NOTE: Try substituting crunchy peanut butter if you'd enjoy a "peanut-tier" taste.

Presto Pesto Pasta

6 servings

Pasta packed with pesto Parmesan flavor. What could be tastier? What could be simpler?!

    1 package (12 ounces) wide egg noodles
    1 jar (8 ounces) pesto sauce
    ¾ cup grated Parmesan cheese

Cook the pasta according to package directions; drain and place in a large bowl. Toss the hot pasta with the pesto sauce until evenly coated. Add the Parmesan cheese and toss again. Serve hot, topped with additional Parmesan cheese, if desired.

NOTE: For a change of pace, try this with tortellini instead of egg noodles. Bottled pesto is available in supermarket produce sections or with the other pasta sauces.

Spaghetti Salad

10 servings

If you think spaghetti is only good teamed with sauce and meatballs, then you'd better think again!

> 1 pound spaghetti, broken in half
> 1 bottle (8 ounces) Italian dressing
> 3 tablespoons salad supreme (see Note)
> ½ cup chopped red onions (1 small onion)
> ½ cup chopped green bell pepper (about 1 large pepper)
> ½ cup chopped red bell pepper (about 1 large pepper)

Cook the spaghetti according to package directions; drain, rinse, and drain again. Place in a large bowl and add the remaining ingredients. Mix well and refrigerate for 2 to 3 hours before serving.

NOTE: Salad supreme, also called salad sprinkle, is a spice blend found in the supermarket spice section.

Cabbage and Noodles

6 to 8 servings

With cabbage so beautiful year-round, this one is sure to become a regular—it is in my house.

> ¼ cup vegetable oil
> 1½ cups coarsely chopped onions (about 2 medium-
> sized onions)
> 4 cups thickly shredded cabbage (about ½ of a
> medium-sized head)
> 1 package (8 ounces) bowtie noodles
> ¼ teaspoon garlic powder
> ½ teaspoon salt
> ¼ teaspoon white pepper

Cook the bowties according to package directions; drain and set aside. Meanwhile, heat the oil in a large skillet over medium-high heat; sauté the onions and cabbage until very soft and lightly browned. Add the remaining ingredients and cook for 7 to 10 minutes, or until heated through. Serve immediately.

Garlic Tortellini

4 to 6 servings

If you love garlic (and I do), then here's a dish for you that's great either hot or cold. And the peppers add a super, colorful crunch.

> 1 bag (16 ounces) frozen cheese tortellini
> 3 tablespoons butter, melted
> 1 cup chopped onions (about 1 medium-sized onion)
> 1 cup chopped red bell pepper (about 2 large
> peppers)
> 1 package (0.65 ounces) cheese garlic salad
> dressing mix

Cook the tortellini according to package directions; drain and place in a medium-sized bowl. Add the melted butter and toss gently to coat the tortellini. Add the remaining ingredients and toss well.

NOTE: Cheese garlic salad dressing mix should be available in your supermarket dressing section.

Spaetzle

4 to 6 servings

Sound complicated? No way! Just mix, spoon, and enjoy. And you thought you couldn't make pasta!

> 3 cups all-purpose flour
> 2 tablespoons dried dillweed or mixed herbs (like dried chives, parsley, and basil)
> 2 teaspoons salt, divided
> ¼ teaspoon pepper
> 4 eggs, beaten
> 1¾ cups milk

In a large bowl, combine the flour, dillweed, 1 teaspoon of the salt, and the pepper. Make a well in the center and pour in the beaten eggs and milk; mix by hand just until smooth. Bring a large pot of water to a hard, rolling boil and add the remaining 1 teaspoon salt. Over the pot, with a wide slotted spoon, scoop out a spoonful of batter and shake it lightly until it breaks into strands that fall into the water; the pieces of batter will congeal to form spaetzle. When the spaetzle float to the top of the water, remove them with the slotted spoon and drain on paper towels. Repeat until no batter remains.

NOTE: Add spaetzle to any soup to make it homemade yummy, serve it with any meat or chicken dish, or simply serve warm spaetzle plain, with butter or gravy, or topped with cheese.

Sicilian Linguine
and Eggplant

6 to 8 servings

*As the end of summer arrives, so does an abundance of garden egg-
plant . . . So here's a super way to help us use up some of this year's
crop in a fresh-tasting side dish that's good hot or cold.*

1 pound linguine
⅔ cup olive oil, divided
1 pound (2 small) eggplant, cut into ½-inch pieces
¾ teaspoon salt
½ teaspoon pepper
¾ teaspoon garlic powder
½ teaspoon dried oregano
2 tomatoes, chopped
2 tablespoons chopped fresh parsley

In a stockpot, cook the linguine according to the package directions. Drain, rinse, and drain again. Place the linguine in a large
bowl and toss with 2 tablespoons of the oil; set aside. In the same
pot, heat the remaining oil over medium-high heat. Sauté the eggplant until lightly browned, about 10 to 12 minutes. Add the salt,
pepper, garlic powder, and oregano, and sauté for an additional 3
to 5 minutes. Add the linguine, tomatoes, and parsley, and toss
gently until heated through. Serve immediately or cover and refrigerate until ready to serve.

*NOTE: You're probably wondering why I suggest you do this in a stock-
pot—it's so that you don't have to use a lot of pots and pans!*

"Lotsa" Pasta

Angelic Pasta

6 to 8 servings

Because angel hair is the thinnest pasta shape, it cooks in no time. So here's a light, garden-fresh-tasting dish that'll go with everything . . . or stand on its own.

> 1 pound angel hair (capellini), or your favorite long,
> thin pasta
> 4 tablespoons olive or vegetable oil
> 3 cloves garlic, minced
> 5 cups diced fresh tomatoes (about 3 large tomatoes)
> 1 teaspoon dried basil
> 1 teaspoon salt
> ½ teaspoon pepper
> ¾ cup ready-to-use (not condensed) chicken broth or
> prepared bouillon
> ⅓ cup grated Parmesan cheese

Cook the pasta according to the package directions; drain and set aside. Meanwhile, heat the oil in a large skillet over medium-high heat. Add the garlic and cook for one minute. Add the tomatoes, basil, salt, and pepper. Cook for 3 minutes. Add the chicken broth and mix just until warmed. Place the mixture in a large bowl and add the hot pasta; toss well with the Parmesan cheese and serve immediately.

NOTE: This is great as is, or you can add some crushed red pepper, hot pepper sauce, or other seasonings if you want. And nothing says you can't use canned, chunky-style tomatoes or add chunks of cooked meat, chicken, or other veggies to make this dish lots of different ways!

Vanishing Veggies

Do you remember your mom always saying, "Eat your vegetables, they're good for you"? I learned to make them disappear because I knew there'd be no dessert till I did! And after all those years of eating all the vegetables on the side of my meat loaf and roast chicken, I guess I learned to really enjoy them. I suppose if Mom knew that, she'd probably have to stifle a big "I told you so!"

The technology and transportation methods of years ago were nowhere near what they are today. Back then we either ate what was in season or had mushy, overcooked canned vegetables. Not anymore!

Today when you walk into the grocery store and pull your cart up to the produce department . . . watch out! The selection is overwhelming, and the quality is like right-from-the-farm. That's because our growing, processing, and transporting methods *have* come so far. Practically year-round, all of us can get fresh corn and asparagus from the other side of the country, not to mention peppers, beets, tomatoes, and other vegetables—just hours after harvesting, too.

In addition to the awesome abundance of fresh produce, we now have super quality canned and frozen products, too. Our choices are incredible, with all the convenience we need today built in—they're quick and easy, and priced right, too. And with canned and frozen vegetables you never have to worry about whether or not something is in season because in your cupboard or freezer, they never go out of season!

Speaking of seasons, I've included a fresh vegetable availability chart in this chapter. Use it as your guide for just what veggies you can expect to see in the market. (Boy, will your family be impressed!)

Regardless of which vegetables you pick to accent your plate and which recipes you choose for preparing them, remember that now it's a pleasure to make your veggies vanish! (And, after all, dessert *is* right around the corner.)

Vanishing Veggies

Vegetable Storage and Cooking Tips

- Don't buy too many fresh vegetables at once because they lose their flavor over time. Try to buy only a week's worth at a time, at the very most.
- Canned and frozen veggies certainly have a longer shelf life than fresh, but be sure to rotate your stock of new and older ones and use the older ones first. (Most unopened frozen vegetables will last for 10 to 12 months.)
- Don't overcook veggies. So many people decide they don't like this or that vegetable because they've never had it cooked properly. If you're uncertain how long to cook fresh vegetables, ask your grocer or watch my television show for tips. I always give fresh produce tips in my Best Food Buys of the Week segments . . . really, I do!

Besides the recipes in this chapter, I've got a few simple ideas for serving vegetables with that straight-from-the-garden taste. These are only suggestions, so mix and match these methods with your favorite veggies. Cooking time will vary, depending upon the vegetables, the size of the pieces, and your personal doneness preference. Give these tips a try, and you'll be surprised at how easy it is to create your own tasty vegetable dishes—without a recipe:

- Boil or steam vegetables until tender, yet still firm. Some of my favorites include corn, broccoli, cauliflower, carrots, peas, and spinach.
- Bake any of the good boiling or steaming veggies (such as carrots, Brussels sprouts, green beans, and corn) in a covered casserole dish with some water or stock. It's like oven steaming.
- Panfry or stir-fry vegetables in a couple of tablespoons of butter or oil in a skillet over medium heat. Try eggplant, mushrooms, onions, green beans, peppers, peapods, and zucchini this

Vanishing Veggies

way, as well as your choice of others. Add a dash of herbs or spices and watch out . . . Mmm!

- Broiled and grilled vegetables are super. Both ways are great to give a rich, nutty flavor to anything from thick tomato slices to yellow summer squash or zucchini, even sliced onions. Just rub a bit of vegetable oil on them with a dash of seasoning, and broil or grill over medium heat until firm yet tender. Of course, you should turn them once to get that even, grilled look (kind of like giving your vegetables a suntan, with the oil acting as the "tanning lotion").

- This is one place I really like to use a microwave oven because it's quick, clean, and does a nice job with many vegetables. Just place the prepared vegetables in a microwave-safe container with a little water, cover, and cook on high power until tender.

VEGETABLE AVAILABILITY CHART

Legend: **P** = Peak Season, **R** = Regular Availability, blank = not available

	JAN	FEB	MAR	APR	MAY	JUN	JUL	AUG	SEP	OCT	NOV	DEC
ASPARAGUS	P	P	P	P	P	R		R	R	R	R	R
BOSTON/BIBB	P	P	P	P	R	R	P	P	P	R	R	R
BROCCOLI	R	R	P	P	P	P	P	P	R	R	R	R
CABBAGE	P	P	P	P	P	P	R	P	P	P	P	P
CARROTS	R	R	R	R	R	R	R	R	R	R	R	R
CAULIFLOWER	P	P	R	R	R	R	R	R	R	R	R	P
CELERY	R	R	R	R	R	R	R	R	R	R	R	R
CORN	P	P	P	P	P	P	R	P	P	P	P	P
CUCUMBERS	P	P	R	P	P	P	P	P	R	R	R	R
EGGPLANT	P	P	P	P	R	R	R	R	R	R	R	P
FRESH HERBS	R	R	R	R	R	R	R	R	R	R	R	R
GARLIC	R	R	R	R	R	R	R	R	R	R	R	R
GREEN PEAS	P	P	P	P	R	R	R	R	R	R	R	R
ICEBERG LETTUCE	P	P	P	P	P	P	P	P	P	P	P	P
LEAF LETTUCE	R	R	R	R	R	R	P	P	P	R	R	R
MUSHROOMS	R	R	R	R	R	R	R	R	R	R	R	R
ONIONS	P	P	P	R	R	R	R	R	P	P	P	P
POTATOES	R	R	R	R	R	R	R	R	R	R	R	R
RADISHES	R	P	P	P	R	R	R	R	R	R	R	R
ROMAINE	R	R	R	R	R	R	R	P	P	P	R	R
SCALLIONS	P	P	P	P	R	R	R	R	R	R	P	P
SPINACH	P	P	R	R	R	R	P	P	P	R	R	R
SUMMER SQUASH	R	R	R	R	P	P	P	R	R	R	R	R
SWEET PEPPERS	P	P	P	P	P	R	R	R	P	P	P	R
SWEET POTATOES	R	R	R	R	R	R	R	R	R	R	P	P
WINTER SQUASH	R	R	R	R	R	R	R	R	R	R	R	R

🛒 REGULAR AVAILABILITY   🛒 PEAK SEASON

Some specialty shops and importers are able to get out-of-season fresh vegetables year-round (though they're usually pricey), so you may be able to find them even when this chart says you shouldn't be able to. Remember: This is only a guide.

Corn on the Cob Tips

Corn on the cob is a favorite way to enjoy one of today's most popular vegetables, and nothing can beat its fresh taste. Here are some winning ways to cook it up so it'll be perfect every time. No matter which way you decide to cook corn on the cob, you should always start with the freshest corn available.

To Boil Bring a stockpot full of cold water to a boil over high heat and add 2 to 3 tablespoons of sugar. Remove the husks and all the silks from the corn, then place the corn in the boiling water. When the water returns to a boil, turn off the heat and let the corn sit in the hot water for about 20 minutes.

To Steam Place 2 inches of water in a stockpot and a steamer or colander in the pot. Bring the water to a boil over high heat. Meanwhile, remove the husks and all the silks from the corn. After the water boils, place the husked corn in the steamer. Cover the pot and steam the corn for 10 to 15 minutes, or until tender. Be careful not to burn yourself when removing the cover.

To Microwave Remove the husks and all the silks from the corn. Place the husked corn in a sealable plastic bag. Add butter and/or salt, pepper, and other desired seasonings. Seal the bag, leaving about 1 inch open. Cook on high power for about 2 minutes per ear. Cooking time may vary, depending upon the wattage of your microwave.

To Oven Roast Preheat the oven to 425°F. Peel back the corn husks and remove the silks, then loosely rewrap the husks around the cobs. Twist the husks to secure. Soak the wrapped cobs in cold water for 10 to 15 minutes, then place them on an oven rack and bake for 18 to 22 minutes, depending on the size. If you would like to keep your oven clean, wrap each ear in aluminum foil before

roasting. This method works well when you have a large quantity of corn to cook at the same time.

NOTES: With each method, cook the corn just until it's tender and steaming. I like it plain, but it's also good served with melted butter, salt, and pepper. You can figure about 1 tablespoon butter per ear of corn, and 1 to 2 ears per person.

One-Dish Veggies

6 servings

One-dish cooking means easy clean-up . . . Now, that's my type of cooking!

>1 can (15 ounces) creamed corn
>1 package (10 ounces) frozen chopped broccoli,
>   cooked and drained
>¾ cup crumbled Ritz-type crackers
>1 egg
>1 tablespoon minced onions
>¼ teaspoon salt
>⅛ teaspoon pepper
>3 tablespoons melted butter or margarine

Preheat the oven to 350°F. Combine all the ingredients in a large bowl. Pour into a 1½-quart casserole dish that has been coated with nonstick vegetable spray. Bake for 35 minutes, until the casserole is golden brown and bubbly.

NOTE: Try adding ½ teaspoon of your favorite spice to "zip" this up—try dill, basil, or garlic!

Carrot Bake

6 to 9 servings

This is so good that the kids won't know how good it is for them. Sshh . . . it'll be our secret!

> 1 pound peeled fresh or frozen carrots, cooked and mashed
> 6 tablespoons softened butter or margarine
> 4 eggs
> 1 cup cracker meal
> ¾ cup milk
> ¾ cup (3 ounces) shredded Cheddar cheese
> 1 tablespoon minced onions
> 1 tablespoon sugar
> 1½ teaspoons dried dillweed
> 2 teaspoons seasoned salt

Preheat the oven to 350°F. Place the mashed carrots in a large bowl; add the butter and mix well. Add the eggs, one at a time, beating after each addition. Stir in the remaining ingredients. Pour the mixture into a greased 1½-quart casserole dish or an 8-inch square baking pan, and bake for 50 to 60 minutes, or until light golden. Let cool for 10 minutes, then run a knife around the inside of the dish; cut into serving-sized pieces and serve.

NOTE: You can bake these in muffin tins for a quick pickup side dish that will get you guaranteed raves. (And the baking time is reduced to one third. Now that's quick and easy!)

Mushroom Crisp

6 servings

Apple crisp and peach crisp better move over and make room for this veggie version that's gonna be a sure hit.

¼ cup (½ stick) butter or margarine
5 cups (¾ pound) sliced mushrooms
2½ cups croutons, divided
1 cup heavy cream
1½ tablespoons prepared steak sauce
¼ teaspoon salt
¼ teaspoon garlic powder

Preheat the oven to 400°F. In a medium-sized skillet, melt the butter, then add the mushrooms and sauté until golden, about 5 minutes. Place 2 cups croutons in a large bowl and mix in the sautéed mushrooms. Place in an 8-inch square baking dish, and top with the remaining croutons. In a small bowl, combine the remaining ingredients and mix until blended. Pour mixture evenly over the entire baking dish and bake for 20 to 25 minutes, or until the top is golden brown.

Jazzy Peas

4 servings

Here's a way to take a simple summer vegetable and jazz it up all year long.

> 1 package (10 ounces) frozen peas
> 2 teaspoons butter
> 1 teaspoon (1 small clove) chopped garlic
> ½ cup chopped onions
> 2 tablespoons ketchup

Prepare the peas according to the package directions; drain. Meanwhile, melt the butter in a small skillet over medium heat and sauté the garlic and onions until golden brown. Stir in the ketchup and peas, and simmer for 5 to 8 minutes, or until hot. Serve immediately.

NOTE: If you prefer, you could use a drained 17-ounce can of peas instead of the frozen ones. You don't even have to heat them first. Just be sure they're heated through after adding them to the skillet.

Baked Green Bean Crunch

4 to 6 servings

*I've found a new way to give some Asian-style crunch to an old favorite.
It'll be gone before you can say "Sayonara."*

      1 can (10¾ ounces) condensed cream of
           mushroom soup
      1 package (16 ounces) frozen green beans
      1 can (8 ounces) sliced water chestnuts, drained
      1 can (2.8 ounces) French-fried onions, divided

Preheat the oven to 350°F. In a large bowl, combine the mushroom
soup, green beans, and water chestnuts. Mix in half of the can of
French-fried onions. Pour into a 7" × 11" glass baking dish that
has been coated with nonstick vegetable spray and bake for 25
minutes. Top with the remaining French-fried onions and bake for
5 more minutes, until the casserole is bubbly and the onions are
light brown on top.

Broiled Garden Tomatoes

6 servings

A fancy vegetable? A special garnish? Either way, it's sure to please everyone.

> 1 can (2.8 ounces) French-fried onions, chopped into
>   coarse crumbs
> ¼ cup grated Parmesan cheese
> 3 firm, medium-sized tomatoes, cut in half
> 1 tablespoon butter or margarine, melted

Preheat the broiler. In a small bowl, combine the onion crumbs and Parmesan cheese. Brush the cut side of the tomatoes with the melted butter. Sprinkle the tomatoes with the onion-cheese mixture, then place on a broiler pan and broil until the tops are lightly browned. Turn off the broiler and close the oven door, leaving the tomatoes inside for 5 to 8 more minutes, or until they are soft but not falling apart.

NOTE: *Try this with fresh garden tomatoes for a real knock-out treat!*

Easy Eggplant

about 6 servings

Eggplant is one of those vegetables that people always shy away from because they think it's too complicated to make . . . well, not anymore!

> 4 tablespoons vegetable oil
> 1 medium-sized (1 to 1½ pounds) eggplant, cut into
>   large chunks
> ⅛ teaspoon salt
> ⅛ teaspoon black pepper
> 2 cloves garlic, crushed
> ¼ cup coarsely chopped scallions or onions
> 1 tablespoon soy sauce
> 1 tablespoon white vinegar
> 1 tablespoon water
> 1 teaspoon sugar

Heat the oil in a large skillet over medium-high heat; sauté the eggplant for about 5 to 8 minutes. Add the salt, pepper, garlic, and scallions and cook for 2 to 3 minutes. Add the soy sauce, vinegar, water, and sugar. Reduce the heat to low and cook for about 10 more minutes, until the eggplant is soft.

NOTE: To make this into an easy ratatouille, just cut a medium-sized zucchini and a medium-sized green bell pepper into chunks and add them along with a 28-ounce can of crushed tomatoes when you add the seasonings.

Tropical Squash

4 servings

Amazing!! This is one of the best squash recipes I've ever made. It's light and flavorful, with a sweet, fruity **OOH it's so GOOD!!**™

> 1 package (12 ounces) frozen butternut squash,
>   thawed
> ½ cup crushed pineapple, drained
> ¼ cup firmly packed brown sugar
> ½ teaspoon ground cinnamon
> 2 egg whites

Preheat the oven to 350°F. Combine all the ingredients in a large bowl and pour into a 1-quart casserole dish that has been coated with nonstick vegetable spray. Bake, covered, for 40 to 45 minutes, or until the center is set.

NOTE: This is like a squash soufflé, so I recommend serving it right out of the oven.

Vegetable Rounds

8 mini-pizzas

Nobody can refuse these, so they're the perfect way to get veggies into any meal. (And they make great snacks, too!)

> 1 package (17.3 ounces) refrigerator buttermilk biscuits (8 biscuits)
> ¼ cup vegetable oil
> ½ cup chopped red bell pepper (about 1 large pepper)
> ½ cup chopped green bell pepper (about 1 large pepper)
> ½ cup chopped onions
> 1 cup sliced mushrooms
> 2 cloves garlic, chopped
> 1 cup (4 ounces) shredded mozzarella cheese

Preheat the oven to 375°F. Flatten out the biscuits on cookie sheets that have been coated with nonstick vegetable spray. In a medium sized skillet, heat the oil over medium-high heat and add the bell peppers, onions, mushrooms, and garlic; cook for about 5 minutes, or until tender but still firm. Top the biscuits with the vegetables and sprinkle with the cheese. Bake for 12 to 15 minutes, until the cheese is bubbly and melted.

NOTE: If you don't have all of these vegetables on hand, substitute what you do have.

Simple Spinach

3 to 4 servings

The name says it all—so simple, so yummy, so muscle-making!

> 1 package (10 ounces) cleaned fresh spinach
> ½ teaspoon garlic powder
> 2 tablespoons olive oil
> ¼ teaspoon salt
> ⅛ teaspoon pepper

Preheat the oven to 350°F. In a large bowl, toss the spinach with the remaining ingredients. Place into a 7" × 11" baking dish and bake for 15 minutes, or until the spinach leaves are wilted.

NOTE: These days most of the packaged spinach we buy is prewashed. It sure saves us time! If your spinach isn't prewashed, be sure to clean it well and dry.

Green Beans Satay

3 to 4 servings

I originally got this recipe from a Thai restaurant, where the chef was kind enough to share it with me, so now I'm sharing my version with you.

1 tablespoon butter or margarine
1 package (9 ounces) frozen cut green beans
1 tablespoon peanut butter
¼ cup sliced almonds
¼ teaspoon salt

In a medium-sized skillet, melt the butter over medium-high heat. Add the green beans and sauté until tender, yet still crisp. Add the remaining ingredients and mix well; continue mixing until heated through and coated evenly. Serve immediately.

NOTE: I don't recommend reheating these if left over, because the peanut butter may separate.

French Onion Pickups

6 to 8 servings

If you love French onion soup, then here's a vegetable pickup that belongs on the side of your plate.

> 2 tablespoons vegetable oil
> 2 medium-sized onions, coarsely chopped
> ¼ cup mayonnaise
> 1 large French bread, split in half lengthwise
> 1 package (6 ounces) Swiss cheese, sliced or shredded

Preheat the broiler. In a large skillet, heat the oil over ·medium-high heat. Add the onions and sauté until nicely browned; set aside. Spread the mayonnaise over the cut sides of the bread and broil about 6 inches from the heat source until light brown and bubbly. Remove from the broiler and cover each side with the onions; top with the cheese and broil for another 2 to 3 minutes, until the cheese is melted. Cut at an angle into generous portions.

NOTE: This makes a great go-along for steak, and it's sure easy enough to cut them into bite-sized pieces for a quick hors d'oeuvre.

Autumn Acorn Squash

4 servings

Cinnamon, maple syrup, and acorn squash—what a natural combination! This was served to me by the best squash maker in the whole world, and I instantly fell in love with its simple richness. (Thanks, Patty!)

2 acorn squash, cut in half lengthwise
1 cup maple or pancake syrup
1 tablespoon butter, melted
1 teaspoon ground cinnamon or nutmeg

Preheat the oven to 400°F. Place the cut squash in a 9″ × 13″ baking dish, cut side up. In a medium-sized bowl, combine the maple syrup, butter, and cinnamon. Coat the cut half of the squash evenly with the syrup mixture, using all of the mixture. Bake for 1 hour, basting occasionally, or until the squash is fork-tender and starts to brown around the edges.

NOTE: Be careful when you check the squash and remove it from the oven, because the syrup is very hot and can burn you!

Snappy Stir-fry

4 servings

Now you can stay home and satisfy your yen for the great tastes of Chinese restaurants—and save some yen while you're at it!

¼ cup peanut oil
2½ cups small fresh broccoli florets (1 medium-sized head)
1 large red bell pepper, cut into ¼-inch strips
1 teaspoon minced garlic (2 cloves)
1 tablespoon soy sauce
¼ teaspoon salt
1 tablespoon sesame seed

In a medium-sized skillet, heat the oil over medium-high heat. Add the broccoli and red pepper and stir-fry for about 3 minutes. Add the garlic, soy sauce, and salt and continue stir-frying for 3 to 5 more minutes, until the broccoli is tender but still crisp. Sprinkle with the sesame seed and serve immediately.

NOTE: To make a successful stir-fry, be sure to continually stir the ingredients throughout the frying.

Texas Corn

6 servings

Did you know that salsa is America's favorite condiment? Well, it is—and here it is, combined with one of America's favorite vegetables to make a side-dish star.

> 2 tablespoons olive oil
> 1 package (16 ounces) frozen corn
> 1 cup salsa
> ½ cup chopped scallions (about 4 scallions)
> 1 can (2.25 ounces) sliced olives (½ cup)

In a medium-sized skillet, heat the oil over medium-high heat. Add the corn and cook, stirring, for about 5 minutes. Add the remaining ingredients, reduce the heat to low, and simmer for another 5 minutes. Serve immediately.

NOTE: You can vary the hotness of this dish by using your choice of mild, medium, or hot salsa.

Cauliflower Steamin' Stir-fry

4 to 6 servings

A stir-fry with no oil?? Believe it! Now you've got a side-dish choice that's great-tasting and good for you, too.

> 1 small head cauliflower, broken into florets
> 1 cup sliced carrots (about 2 carrots)
> ⅔ cup ready-to-use (not condensed) chicken broth, divided
> 1 cup sliced fresh mushrooms
> 4 scallions, cut into 1-inch pieces
> 1 teaspoon minced galic (2 cloves)
> 1 tablespoon soy sauce
> Pinch of sugar

In a large skillet, "sauté" the cauliflower and carrots in ⅓ cup chicken broth over medium-high heat for 4 to 5 minutes. Add the mushrooms, scallions, and garlic and continue cooking for another 5 minutes. In a small bowl, combine the remaining ⅓ cup chicken broth, the soy sauce, and the sugar. Pour over the cauliflower mixture, reduce the heat to low and simmer, covered, for 10 to 12 minutes, until the cauliflower is fork tender.

NOTE: If you'd like to turn this into a complete meal, just add pieces of leftover cooked chicken or beef during the last 5 minutes of cooking and serve it over steamed rice.

Peppery Carrots with Dill

4 to 5 servings

Sometimes the simple things are the best, and this recipe is the proof!

> 1 bag (1 pound) fresh carrots
> 2 tablespoons butter
> ¼ teaspoon dried dillweed
> ¼ teaspoon salt
> ¼ teaspoon pepper

Peel the carrots, then slice into sticks about 3 inches long. Place the carrots in a medium-sized saucepan and cover with water; bring to a boil. Boil for about 10 minutes, or until tender. Drain the carrots and return them to the pot. Add the remaining ingredients and cook over low heat until the butter is melted and the carrots are evenly coated.

NOTE: The cooking time may vary, depending upon the size and age of the carrots.

Italian-Style Zucchini

8 servings

A friend of mine once said, "Don't plant zucchini unless you have lots of friends and family to share them with!" So here's a flavorful way to use up that abundant summer crop.

> ½ cup mayonnaise
> ¼ teaspoon onion powder
> ¼ teaspoon salt
> ⅛ teaspoon pepper
> ⅛ teaspoon garlic powder
> 2 tablespoons Italian-flavored bread crumbs
> 4 medium-sized zucchini

Preheat the oven to 350°F. In a small bowl, combine all the ingredients except the zucchini; mix well and set aside. Trim the ends of the zucchini and cut each in half lengthwise. With a fork, score the cut side of each zucchini half about ¼ inch deep, and brush evenly with the mayonnaise mixture. Place cut side up on a cookie sheet and bake for 20 minutes, or until golden and fork tender.

NOTE: Yellow summer squash will work well in place of the zucchini, if you prefer.

Bavarian Cabbage

8 servings

When I was a boy, I used to love eating corned beef and cabbage with a crusty piece of rye bread at my neighbor's house, and every time I taste this, the memory comes right back to me.

    1 medium-sized cabbage
    1½ cups water
    1 teaspoon salt
    ¼ teaspoon pepper
    ¼ cup (½ stick) butter
    ½ teaspoon caraway seed

Preheat the oven to 350°F. Cut the cabbage into 8 wedges and place in a 9″ × 13″ baking dish. Add the water to the dish, sprinkle the cabbage with the salt and pepper, and cover tightly with aluminum foil. Bake for about 40 minutes, or to desired tenderness. Remove to a serving platter. Place the butter and caraway seed in a small, microwaveable bowl and microwave on high power for 40 to 50 seconds, or until melted. Pour over the steamed cabbage. Serve hot.

NOTE: If you don't care for the taste of caraway seed—no problem. You can still make this . . . but make it Garden Fresh Cabbage and substitute 1½ teaspoons chopped fresh basil or ¾ teaspoon dried basil for the caraway seed.

Creamy Onions

4 to 5 servings

Okay, okay, you don't like the usual strong taste of onions. But made this way—so mellow and creamy—you're sure to have a change of heart.

> 1 tablespoon butter or margarine
> 2 medium-sized onions, peeled and cut into wedges
> 1 can (10¾ ounces) condensed cream of
>   mushroom soup
> ⅓ cup milk
> ¼ teaspoon ground nutmeg

Melt the butter in a medium-sized skillet over medium-high heat; sauté the onions for 10 to 15 minutes, until they soften and start to brown. In a small bowl, combine the remaining ingredients, mixing well. Add to the skillet, reduce heat, and simmer for 5 to 8 minutes.

NOTE: For an extra-fancy side dish, use 1 package (16 ounces) frozen pearl onions, thawed and drained.

Carrot Pancakes

about 16 pancakes

If you think carrots are only for rabbits and pancakes are only for break-fast, well . . . think again!

> ½ cup grated Parmesan cheese
> ⅔ cup all-purpose flour
> 1 teaspoon baking powder
> 8 eggs
> 2 teaspoons vegetable oil
> 1 teaspoon salt
> ½ teaspoon pepper
> ¼ cup finely chopped onions or finely sliced scallions
> 4 cups (2 pounds) shredded carrots (lightly packed)

Combine all the ingredients in a large bowl. Mix with an electric beater until well combined. Coat a griddle or large skillet with nonstick vegetable spray and heat over medium-high heat. For each pancake, ladle ¼ cup pancake batter onto the hot griddle and cook for 3 to 4 minutes on each side, until the insides are dry and the outsides are golden brown.

Northern Chili Beans

3 to 4 servings

You've heard of "East meets West"... Well, now Northern beans meet Southern flavor—and the results are awesome.

> 1 can (15.5 to 16 ounces) Great Northern beans,
>   rinsed and drained
> 1 cup salsa
> 2 tablespoons honey
> ¼ teaspoon chili powder

Combine all the ingredients in a medium-sized saucepan. Bring to a boil over medium heat, then immediately reduce the heat to low. Continue heating, stirring occasionally, for 5 to 7 minutes, until the mixture is thoroughly heated through.

NOTE: Remember that you can always change the hotness of this one by going to a milder or a hotter salsa... Now that's the easiest way I know to increase or decrease the spice in your life!

Sweet-and-Sour
Red Cabbage

3 to 4 servings

I just found the best go-along for meat and poultry. I know you'll enjoy these great Old World flavors!

> 2 tablespoons vegetable oil
> 2 tablespoons white vinegar
> ¼ cup sugar
> 1 teaspoon caraway seed
> ¼ cup water
> 4 cups (½ of a medium-sized head) shredded cabbage

In a large skillet, heat all the ingredients, except the cabbage, over medium heat, stirring constantly for 2 minutes. Add the cabbage and stir to coat. Reduce the heat to low, cover, and simmer for 20 minutes.

NOTE: For a special taste treat, substitute apple cider vinegar for the white vinegar.

Stuffed Peppers

4 servings

These are so hearty that everybody'll be asking for seconds!

2 bell peppers, split lengthwise and cleaned
¼ cup olive oil
1 medium-sized onion, chopped
4 cloves garlic, minced
1 ripe tomato, finely chopped
4 to 5 anchovies, chopped, *or* ¼ teaspoon salt
¼ cup chopped fresh parsley
½ cup dry bread crumbs
2 tablespoons white wine
¼ teaspoon black pepper
Grated Parmesan cheese for sprinkling (optional)

Preheat the oven to 350°F. Fill a medium-sized saucepan half full with water and bring to a boil. Carefully place the pepper halves in the boiling water and boil for 4 to 5 minutes, just until they begin to soften. Remove the peppers from the boiling water and plunge into cold water; drain and set aside. In a large skillet, heat the olive oil over medium heat. Add the onions and garlic and sauté just until softened; do not burn. Remove from the heat and add the remaining ingredients except the pepper halves and the Parmesan cheese. Mix well. Fill the peppers evenly with the mixture and place in a greased 8″ × 11″ baking dish. Sprinkle with the Parmesan cheese, if desired. Bake for 20 minutes.

NOTE: Try stuffing mushroom halves, hollowed-out zucchini, garden fresh tomatoes . . . The possibilities are endless. When using these types of vegetables, you don't have to boil them first. Now that's easy!

Hearty Hodgepodge

Hearty Hodgepodge

What should we have with dinner that isn't a potato, rice, or
Hey, I've got it! Spicy Corn Stuffing (page 115) . . . or maybe
Polenta (page 123) . . . or how 'bout Beefy Barley (page 117)
you'll fall in love with these recipes in no time.

With this chapter I'm filling your plate with pizzazz, like
stuffing that has a . . . well, let's say a new twist (Pretzel Stu
page 124). And I'm also sharing some ideas from the rest
world, like Polish Pierogi (page 121), and even a New Mexican
on Middle Eastern couscous (page 119). I also have a few i
that'll have you asking yourself, "Why haven't I ever served
before?" I think if you haven't, maybe it's because you ha
thought of them at all, or you thought they were too much w
Well, **my** way they aren't!

So here they are—quick, unique, and tasty side dishes that
give you all new, different ways to be a kitchen hero. Hooray!

Spicy Corn Stuffing

4 to 6 servings

When dinner needs a hearty, "pick-me-up" side dish, this spicy corn stuffing is perfect! And with a touch of hot pepper, it's sure to be an eye opener.

> 3 cups cornbread or corn muffin crumbs (made from prepared cornbread or store-bought muffins)
> ⅓ cup chopped onions
> 3 eggs, lightly beaten
> ⅓ cup water
> ⅛ teaspoon cayenne pepper
> ½ teaspoon salt
> ¼ teaspoon black pepper

Preheat the oven to 350°F. In a large bowl, mix together all of the ingredients and pour into an 8-inch pie dish that has been coated with nonstick vegetable spray. Bake for 25 minutes, or until the center is firm.

NOTE: This stuffing is great with gravy, and can also be used to stuff a roasting chicken or a small turkey.

Dimple Dumplings

10 to 12 dumplings

Do you remember those dumplings cooking at the top of Mom's big pot of beef stew? Now you can have them on the side of your favorite dinner—and with each bite comes a big smile to show off your dimples!

> 3 quarts water
> 2 cups biscuit baking mix
> ⅔ cup milk
> 1 teaspoon dried dillweed
> Pinch of salt
> Pinch of pepper

Bring the water to a boil in a soup pot. Meanwhile, place all the remaining ingredients in a large bowl; mix by hand until well blended. Put a heaping tablespoon of dough into the boiling water. Repeat until all the dough is used up. Cover the pot tightly, reduce the heat to low, and simmer for 12 to 15 minutes, until the dumplings are shiny white.

NOTE: Top these off with melted butter or your favorite homemade or bottled gravy.

Beefy Barley

8 servings

All too often we serve the same potato, rice, or stuffing side dishes. Why not give yourself and your family a pleasant change of pace with barley?

> 4 cups ready-to-use (not condensed) beef broth
> 1 cup barley, not quick or instant
> ½ teaspoon ground cumin
> ¼ teaspoon black pepper
> 1 tablespoon vegetable oil
> 1 cup chopped onions (about 1 medium-sized onion)
> 1 cup chopped red or green bell pepper (about
>   1 medium-sized pepper)

In a medium-sized saucepan, bring the beef broth to a boil. Add the barley, cumin, and black pepper. Reduce the heat to low, cover, and simmer for 45 to 50 minutes, or until the barley is tender and all of the liquid is absorbed. Remove the saucepan from the heat and set aside. In a small skillet, heat the oil over medium-high heat. Sauté the onions and pepper until soft and lightly browned; add to the cooked barley. Mix well and serve.

NOTE: If you're not going to serve this right away, it can be reheated in the microwave. Or, place it in a 1½-quart casserole dish that has been coated with nonstick vegetable spray, cover, and refrigerate. When ready to serve, preheat the oven to 325°F. and heat the covered barley casserole for 20 to 25 minutes, or until completely hot.

Hearty Hodgepodge

Baked Bean Fritters

3 dozen

Baked Bean Fritters?? I know, it sounds crazy ... but try 'em. They'll make a believer out of you, too!

>   1¾ cups all-purpose flour
>   2 teaspoons baking powder
>   1 teaspoon salt
>   ½ teaspoon black pepper
>   4 eggs
>   2 cans (16 ounces each) baked beans, rinsed and
>   drained
>   ½ cup chopped green bell pepper
>   ½ cup chopped onions
>   1 tablespoon brown sugar
>   1 teaspoon garlic powder
>   1 cup vegetable oil

In a large bowl, combine the flour, baking powder, salt, and eggs until well blended. Add the remaining ingredients, except the oil. Heat the oil in a large skillet over medium-high heat. Drop the batter by teaspoonfuls into the oil; when the sides of the fritters begin to bubble, after about 1 minute, turn the fritters and brown the other sides. When golden brown and crispy on all sides, remove the fritters and place on paper towels to drain. Repeat until all the batter is used.

NOTE: After the fritters are drained, keep them hot in a 300°F. oven (on a baking sheet) until the whole batch is finished cooking.

New Mexican Couscous

6 to 8 servings

A perfect example of how the blending of cultures really works—Mediterranean couscous tossed with a few Southwestern touches . . . It makes a super blend!

⅔ cup uncooked couscous
½ cup sour cream
1 can (8 ounces) whole kernel corn, drained
1 can (15 ounces) pinto beans, rinsed and drained
2 ripe tomatoes, chopped
1 can (4½ ounces) chopped green chilies
1 tablespoon chopped fresh parsley
1½ teaspoons ground cumin
1 cup (4 ounces) shredded Cheddar cheese

Preheat the oven to 350°F. Prepare the couscous according to package directions. In a large bowl, combine all the ingredients except the cheese; mix well. Place the mixture into a 1½-quart casserole dish that has been coated with nonstick vegetable spray. Bake for 20 to 25 minutes, or until heated through. Remove from the oven and sprinkle with the cheese. Continue baking for 5 to 7 more minutes, or until the cheese is melted.

NOTE: Usually found in your supermarket rice section, couscous is becoming a very popular item these days.

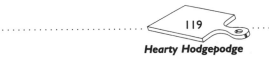

Citrus Stuffing

6 servings

Citrus and stuffing—this sweet, refreshing combination is just one more way to enjoy one of our favorite side dishes. (And this one's even sweeter because it's so easy!)

> 1 package (6 to 8 ounces) stuffing mix
> ½ cup apricot preserves, divided
> 1 can (11 ounces) mandarin oranges, drained
> ½ cup chopped walnuts, divided

Preheat the oven to 350°F. Prepare the stuffing according to the package directions and, while still warm, stir in ¼ cup of the apricot preserves. Pour half of the mixture into a 9" × 5" loaf pan that has been coated with nonstick vegetable spray. Spread the oranges over the mixture and sprinkle with ¼ cup of the chopped nuts. Cover with the remaining stuffing mixture; spread the remaining ¼ cup preserves evenly over the stuffing and top with the remaining nuts. Bake for 25 minutes and serve immediately.

NOTE: Any brand of stuffing mix will work fine . . . you know, the quick stuffing mixes with all the spices included.

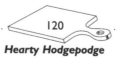

Pierogi

4 servings

If you've ever had pierogi for dinner, you might have thought that they would make a great side dish, too. Well, they do . . . they do!

> 1 package (16.9 ounces) frozen pierogi
> 2 tablespoons butter
> 1 cup chopped onions (about 1 small onion)
> 1 teaspoon dried dillweed
> Pinch of salt
> Pinch of black pepper

In a large saucepan of boiling water, cook the pierogi, uncovered, for 3 to 5 minutes. Drain and set aside. In the same saucepan, melt the butter over medium-high heat. Sauté the onions for 10 to 15 minutes, or until golden brown. Add the remaining ingredients, including the cooked pierogi, and gently stir until the pierogi are heated through and coated with the onion. Serve immediately.

NOTE: Pierogi originated in Poland, but their destination is your belly, so try making them as above, or substitute your favorite spices and herbs to give them different ethnic accents.

Granola Stuffing

6 to 8 servings

Wow! Nature's natural granola accenting this year's holiday stuffing! They may not know what's in it, but they'll surely know they want seconds—so you'd better make a double batch!

2¼ cups water
¼ cup (½ stick) butter or margarine
¼ cup honey
½ cup raisins (optional)
¼ teaspoon poultry seasoning
1 bag (8 ounces) seasoned stuffing cubes (not stuffing mix)
2 cups granola
2 eggs, beaten

Preheat the oven to 350°F. In a large saucepan, combine the water, butter, honey, raisins, and poultry seasoning. Bring to a boil, then remove from the heat. Add the stuffing and granola and mix well. Add the beaten eggs and mix well. Turn into an 8-inch square baking dish that has been coated with nonstick vegetable spray. Bake for 25 minutes, until the top is browned.

NOTE: If you have meat cooking at the same time at a lower temperature, you can bake this at 325°F. for 35 to 40 minutes. And if your granola already has raisins in it, then omit the ½ cup raisins listed above.

Italian Polenta

6 servings

Polenta used to be a specialty of Northern Italy. But with its hearty rich flavor, the word spread across the Atlantic . . . and now you can find out why!

> 4 cups water
> ¼ cup (½ stick) butter
> 2 teaspoons salt
> 2 cups yellow cornmeal

In a large nonstick saucepan, bring the water, butter, and salt to a boil. Slowly stir in the cornmeal with a wooden spoon. Reduce the heat to low and continue stirring constantly until the mixture is firm. Cover and cook without stirring for 15 to 20 minutes more, or until thick and the sides pull away from the pan. Serve immediately.

NOTE: If you use a nonstick saucepan, when set this will turn right out onto your serving platter. If it should lump a little when you add the cornmeal, stir with a wire whisk for 1 minute, or until the lumps break up. If there are leftovers that harden, cut into ½-inch slices and panfry in a little butter or oil.

Pretzel Stuffing

6 to 8 servings

Pretzels in stuffing?! You betcha! As crazy as it sounds, it's a gangbuster stuffing that the kids will love . . . okay, the adults will, too!

> 10 ounces (about 3 cups) salted pretzel sticks,
>   broken into pieces
> 2 cups hot water
> 3 eggs
> 1 cup sour cream
> 1 teaspoon onion powder

Preheat the oven to 350°F. In a medium-sized bowl, soak the pretzels in the hot water for 5 to 7 minutes, until softened. Do not drain. Add the eggs, sour cream, and onion powder and mix well. Pour into a 1½-quart casserole dish that has been coated with nonstick vegetable spray. Bake for 30 to 40 minutes, or until firm in the center.

NOTE: If you like a less salty stuffing, use unsalted pretzels.

Bold Cold Salads

Most of us have our one or two favorite cold salads that we make over and over for every picnic, potluck dinner, and family gathering. We don't bother making them for other times 'cause they seem to take so much work (even though the raves are usually well worth it).

But cold salads are only for summer, you say? Not so! Why not make a batch of "Grate" Carrot Salad (page 131) for your next tailgate party? Or Sweet Potato Salad (page 135) to go along with Thanksgiving dinner? Or what about Confetti Vegetable Salad (page 134) for New Year's Eve, or Presto Potato Salad (page 133) for the perfect addition to your Super Bowl party?

Boy, have I got a bunch of easy, fun recipes for you that will be sure, anytime winners. Don't miss out on all these great year-round side dish possibilities!

Go ahead and give them a try. . . . You'll have fun because not only are they great recipes, but cold means less work at serving time. Yes, less work *and* big flavor. That could only mean . . . **OOH it's so GOOD!!**™

Bold Cold Salads

Serving Tips for Bolder, Colder Salads

- To give that just-made fresh taste to all your prepared salads, always toss or stir them just before serving. As they sit, salads absorb much of their mayonnaise or dressing, so salads made in advance may need a bit more dressing mixed in just before serving.
- If you plan to "fancy up" your cold side dishes or take them to a picnic, leave the garnishing until right before serving. Remember: It's better to have no garnish than wilted garnish.
- Before storing cold, bold salads in the refrigerator, cover them tightly so that they don't pick up tastes from other items.
- Why not send some leftover cold salad to school or the office as a lunchbox go-along? Just pack it in a small insulated container to keep it chilled.
- If you plan to take along a side dish in hot weather, pack it carefully in a cooler with ice to keep it from spoiling.
- If serving any of these fun salads outside, try to avoid placing them in direct sunlight, and put out small amounts at a time in small serving bowls to avoid spoilage.
- Put a date on the storage container so you know when it was made. Remember: Fresh is best.

"Quickie" Marinated Cucumbers

6 to 8 servings

It used to take such a long time to make pickles, but these don't need any special pickling spices, and they're done in a few hours!

¼ cup hot water
⅓ cup sugar
1 bottle (8 ounces) Italian dressing
3 medium-sized cucumbers, cut into ⅛-inch slices
1 medium-sized onion, thinly sliced

In a medium-sized bowl, combine the hot water, sugar, and Italian dressing. Add the cucumbers and onions. Mix well, cover, and chill for at least 2 to 3 hours before serving.

NOTE: The longer you let these marinate, the more flavorful they become. But if you like them really crispy, then you'd better plan to eat them up within a day (which should be no problem since they're so fresh-tasting!).

Tropical Coleslaw

8 to 10 servings

If you bring this to the next family gathering, watch out! 'Cause from then on they'll ask you to bring this tropical dish with you to all the upcoming family outings.

> 10 to 12 cups chopped cabbage (1 large head)
> 2½ cups mayonnaise
> 1 can (20 ounces) crushed pineapple, drained
> 1 cup shredded carrots (about 4 carrots)
> 1 cup chopped red onions (about 1 medium-sized
>   onion)
> ½ teaspoon salt
> ½ teaspoon pepper

In a large bowl, toss all the ingredients until well mixed and evenly coated. Cover and chill for 1 to 2 hours and mix again before serving.

NOTE: You can eliminate the hour(s) of chilling if you're in a rush, but that time really does help the flavors to "marry."

Great Garbanzo Salad

6 servings

What could be better than this terrific, high-energy combination of beans, pasta, and fresh vegetables?

1 can (16 to 20 ounces) garbanzo beans (chick peas),
    rinsed and drained
⅓ cup olive oil
2 tablespoons lemon juice
2 tablespoons chopped fresh parsley
1 teaspoon dried oregano
1 teaspoon salt
½ teaspoon pepper
4 ounces (1 cup) elbow macaroni, uncooked
2 cups cubed fresh tomatoes (about 2 medium-sized
    tomatoes)
1 cup diced celery (1 to 2 celery stalks)
½ cup diced red onions

In a large bowl, combine the garbanzo beans, oil, lemon juice, parsley, oregano, salt, and pepper. Cover and place in the refrigerator to marinate for about 1 hour. Cook the pasta according to package directions and drain. Add to the marinated garbanzo bean mixture, along with the remaining ingredients. Toss well to blend. Serve immediately or cover and chill until ready to serve.

NOTE: If you don't have fresh parsley, use 2 teaspoons of dried parsley flakes.

Bold Cold Salads

"Grate" Carrot Salad

6 to 8 servings

Carrots are included in lots of other salads, but I think it's time to feature them. So in this recipe, carrots are the stars.

 ¾ cup mayonnaise
 2½ tablespoons honey
 ½ teaspoon salt
 4 cups grated carrots (about 8 carrots)
 ½ cup raisins

In a large bowl, combine the mayonnaise, honey, and salt. Add the carrots and mix well, then stir in the raisins.

NOTE: I've found the food processor to be the best and fastest way to grate the carrots, but a hand grater will work just as well if a food processor isn't available.

Everything Coleslaw

about 4 cups

Everybody has his or her own opinion of the best time to have coleslaw—some have to have it at a picnic, some say it's a must with barbecued spareribs, and others insist on having it with fried chicken. Well, here's my no-fail recipe that'll give everyone a chance to decide on their own perfect main-dish match.

>1 cup mayonnaise
>Juice of 1 large lemon
>3 tablespoons sugar
>½ teaspoon celery seed
>1 teaspoon salt
>¼ teaspoon white pepper
>6 cups shredded cabbage (1 small head)
>1 cup shredded carrots (about 2 carrots)

In a large bowl, combine the mayonnaise, lemon juice, sugar, celery seed, salt, and pepper. Add the shredded cabbage and carrots; toss to coat well. Cover and chill for 2 to 3 hours before serving.

NOTE: Some say coleslaw should be sweet, others say it should be tangy. Well, it's easy to adjust the amount of sugar to your own liking to make it your very own taste. You can also use two 10-ounce packages of pre-shredded coleslaw instead of shredding the cabbage and carrots yourself. It's a nice time-saver when you have little preparation time!

Presto Potato Salad

about 4 cups

This may look like a lot of ingredients, but I'll bet you already have them all at your fingertips. And it's a snap to make . . . That's why I call it "Presto"!

> 2 pounds (about 5 large) potatoes, peeled and cut
>   into medium-sized cubes
> 2 cups mayonnaise
> 2 hard-boiled eggs, chopped
> ½ cup diced onions (about 1 small onion)
> 1 cup chopped celery (1 to 2 celery stalks)
> 3 teaspoons prepared yellow mustard
> 2 teaspoons salt
> 1 teaspoon pepper
> ½ teaspoon white vinegar
> 1 tablespoon sweet relish
> 1 teaspoon paprika for sprinkling

Cook the potatoes in a large pot of boiling salted water until just fork-tender, about 20 minutes. (Be careful not to overcook them.) Drain the potatoes, then place in a large bowl, cover, and chill. In a medium-sized bowl, combine the remaining ingredients, then add to the chilled potatoes. Mix well, then sprinkle with the paprika. Salad should be served chilled.

NOTE: I've learned that if you mix the mayonnaise mixture with the potatoes while they're still warm, you'll get a bigger, richer flavor.

Bold Cold Salads

Confetti Vegetable Salad

1¼ cups

"Wow!" "Super-duper!" "Awesome!" These are just a few of the comments you'll hear when you serve this colorful side dish.

>1 green bell pepper, cut into 1-inch chunks
>1 red bell pepper, cut into 1-inch chunks
>1 small head cauliflower, cut into small florets
>1 red onion, cut into 1-inch chunks
>1 pint cherry tomatoes
>1 cup whole green or black olives, drained
>¾ cup Italian dressing
>¼ cup honey
>¼ cup water

In a large bowl, combine the bell peppers, cauliflower, onions, tomatoes, and olives; set aside. In a small bowl, combine the Italian dressing, honey, and water, mixing well. Pour over the vegetables and toss to coat. Cover and chill for 2 hours or overnight, tossing occasionally. Serve chilled.

NOTE: Don't be afraid to mix and match this with your favorite vegetables. Remember: There are no rules.

Sweet Potato Salad

about 4 cups

No, no, no! It's not a misprint. I do mean Sweet Potato Salad. Why not? With their goodness and their growing popularity, why not just find more ways to enjoy them?

> 2 pounds (4 to 5) sweet potatoes, peeled and cut into
>   medium-sized chunks
> 1 cup mayonnaise
> ¼ cup honey
> 1 tablespoon prepared mustard
> ½ cup chopped walnuts
> ¼ teaspoon salt

Cook the potatoes in a medium-sized pot of boiling water for 12 to 15 minutes or until fork-tender. Drain well and place in a large bowl. In a small bowl, combine the remaining ingredients. Pour over the sweet potatoes and mix until they are well coated. Chill before serving.

Honey Mustard
Potato Salad

4 to 5 servings

My viewers always write in and ask for clever potato salad recipes. Well, here's one I got from Idaho and since Idaho is potato country, you know it's got to be great!

> 2 pounds (6 to 7) red potatoes with skins on, washed
> 1 cup mayonnaise
> ⅛ cup honey
> 1 tablespoon prepared mustard
> ¼ teaspoon salt
> ¼ cup sliced scallions (1 to 2 scallions)

In a large saucepan, cook the potatoes in boiling water for 15 to 20 minutes, until fork-tender. Drain and cool, then cut into 1-inch cubes, leaving the skin on. Place in a large bowl. In a small bowl, combine the mayonnaise, honey, mustard, and salt; mix well. Toss the dressing with the potatoes until well coated. Gently toss with the sliced scallions and chill until ready to serve.

Fruit Festival

Fresh fruit . . . Ahh, how I love fresh fruit. Growing up in the Northeast, I couldn't wait for summer so I could have my pick of fresh local summer fruit. That was the only time we could get a variety of fresh produce.

I still have that passion for fruit. And am I lucky! Because today our supermarkets around the country stock California strawberries and even New Zealand kiwis year-round . . . not to mention pears, plums, Florida grapefruit, Finger Lakes and California grapes, Washington apples . . . and on and on! WOW! We're *all* lucky!

Let's not forget the high quality canned and frozen fruit we have available now, too. Both are processed within hours of harvest. That sure gives us a fruit-stand taste with off-the-shelf convenience that wasn't possible when I was a kid.

As in the vegetable chapter, I've got a seasonal availability chart included here. It should give your menu planning and buying a real boost. Why not take all the help we can get to add a variety of fresh fruit to our everyday diets? After all, we like to be creative with our fresh treats, too!

And since we do, I've got some nifty ideas for fruit in this chapter. And no matter whether you're eating a banana right out of its skin, or a mandarin orange in a fancy salad, the taste, the texture, the memories sure will guarantee big smiles and at least a few exclamations of **OOH it's so GOOD!!**™

Fruit Festival

Serving Fancy Fresh Fruit

Instead of just a recipe or two with fresh fruit, I thought it'd be more fun to give you some serving ideas for fruit concoctions. So, have fun and enjoy a festival of fruit on the side, 'cause it adds a burst of color and flavor every time!

- Layer fresh sections of oranges and grapefruit in a glass bowl and top with a bit of orange juice and ginger ale.
- Cut a grapefruit in half, sprinkle each half evenly with a teaspoon of sugar, and broil for 10 to 15 minutes, until hot. Serve each half topped with a maraschino cherry.
- Cut chunks of garden melons, like cantaloupe, honeydew, and seeded watermelon. Toss together to make a fruit salad with lots of pizzazz and juicy freshness.
- Alternate melon chunks with strawberries on a 6-inch bamboo skewer and serve on the side of a luncheon or dinner plate.
- Cut up fresh peaches and toss with a bit of peach liqueur. (Watch out! This one's for adults only!)
- You know those grapes that fall off the bunch and sit in the bowl unwanted? Clean them off and toss them with wedges of fresh apple and a bit of lemonade for a real autumn favorite.
- Here's a simple one: Fan out wedges of seasonal fruit (including melons) on a platter and serve topped with fresh berries as a great breakfast side dish.
- Place blueberries, raspberries, and strawberries in a glass bowl and add a bit of half-and-half and a sprinkle of sugar. Toss to coat.
- Cut a pineapple in half, top to bottom, and hollow out the "meat." Cut that into chunks and place them back into the pineapple cavity.
- For fancy gatherings, make a watermelon basket and fill it with an assortment of fresh-cut fruit. It can even double as a table centerpiece instead of flowers. (It's pretty *and* edible, so it gets *my* vote!)

Fruit Festival

FRUIT AVAILABILITY CHART

Legend: **R** = Regular Availability, **P** = Peak Season

	JAN	FEB	MAR	APR	MAY	JUN	JUL	AUG	SEP	OCT	NOV	DEC
APPLES	P	P	P	P	P	R	R	R	P	P	P	P
BANANAS	R	R	R	R	R	R	R	R	R	R	R	R
BLACKBERRIES		R	R	R		R	R	R				
BLUEBERRIES					R	R	P	P	P	R		
CANTALOUPE	R	R	R	R	P	P	P	P	P	R	R	R
CHERRIES	R	R		R	R	P	P	R				R
GRAPEFRUIT	P	P	P	R	R	R	R	R	R	R	R	P
GRAPES	R	R	R	R	P	P	P	P	P	P	P	R
HONEYDEW	R	R	R	P	P	P	P	P	P	P	R	R
LEMONS	R	R	R	R	P	P	P	R	R	R	R	R
LIMES	P	R	R	R	R	R	P	P	P	P	P	P
SPECIALTY MELONS	R	R	R	R	P	P	P	P	P	R	R	R
NECTARINES	P	P	R	R	R	R	P	P	P	R	R	P
ORANGES	R	P	P	P	P	R	R	R	R	R	P	P
PEACHES	P	P	R	R	R	P	R	R	R	R	R	P
PEARS	R	R	R	R					R	R	R	R
PINEAPPLE	P	P	P	P	P	R	P	P	P	R	R	R
PLANTAINS	R	R	R	R	R	R	R	R	R	R	R	R
PLUMS	P	R	R	R	R	R	R	R	R	P	P	P
RASPBERRIES		R	R	R			R	R	R			
STRAWBERRIES	R	R	P	P	P	R	R	R			R	R
TANGERINES	R	R	R	R						R	R	R
TOMATOES	P	P	P	P	P	R	R	R	R	P	P	P
WATERMELON	R	R	P	P	P	P	P	P	R	R	R	R

🛒 REGULAR AVAILABILITY   🛒 PEAK SEASON

Some specialty shops and importers are able to get out-of-season fresh fruit year-round (though it's usually pricey), so you may be able to find it even when this chart says you shouldn't be able to. Remember: This is only a guide.

Cranberry Bake

2 cups

If you want the taste of fresh-made cranberry sauce but don't have the time . . . look no more.

> 1 can (16 ounces) whole-berry cranberry sauce
> 1 can (11 ounces) mandarin oranges, drained
> ½ teaspoon lemon juice
> 2 teaspoons sugar

Preheat the oven to 350°F. In a medium-sized bowl, combine all the ingredients. Pour into a 1-quart casserole dish that has been coated with nonstick vegetable spray and bake for 20 to 25 minutes, or until the cranberries are hot and bubbly.

NOTE: If you'd like it to be more on the tart side, go ahead and double the amount of lemon juice.

143

Fruit Festival

Ivory Peaches

12 servings

When I travel around the country, viewers often share secret family recipes with me. After you taste this "secret," you'll feel like one of the family, too.

> 1 can (28 ounces) peach slices in heavy syrup
> 1 package (4-serving size) lemon-flavor gelatin mix
> ⅔ cup cream-style cottage cheese
> ½ cup chopped pecans
> 1 pint (2 cups) heavy cream, whipped
> 1 cup miniature marshmallows

Drain the peaches and reserve 1 cup of syrup. In a small saucepan, bring the reserved peach syrup to a boil. Add the gelatin mix and stir until completely dissolved. Cool until slightly thickened. Place the gelatin mixture in a large bowl and fold in the cottage cheese, peach slices, and pecans. Fold in the whipped cream and the marshmallows. Pour into a 2-quart serving bowl and chill for at least 3 hours before serving so that it will firm up.

NOTE: If you want to use regular-sized marshmallows, just cut them into quarters.

Fresh Applesauce

3 to 4 servings

As the summer comes to an end and the air in the North begins to get that crisp chill, that means APPLE SEASON! So what better way to make the season last than to make fresh applesauce?!

8 Granny Smith or other tart fresh apples
½ cup sugar
¾ cup water
¼ teaspoon ground nutmeg (optional)
Dash ground cinnamon (optional)
1 teaspoon grated lemon peel (optional)

Peel and core the apples; cut into thin slices and place in a large pot. Add the sugar and water. Bring to a boil, then mix in the spices, if desired; reduce the heat to a simmer, cover, and cook for 50 to 60 minutes, stirring occasionally.

NOTE: Cooking time can vary, depending on the texture you like—for chunky applesauce, cook it less; for smooth applesauce, cook it more. And if your apples aren't really juicy, you may need to add a bit more water during the simmering to prevent scorching.

Skillet Plantains

4 to 6 servings

You may ask, "What's a plantain?" Well, it's a fruit that's super popular in the South and in South and Central American cultures, too. I'm sure it will soon win a place at your table . . . really!

> ¼ cup (½ stick) butter
> 2 large plantains, peeled and sliced diagonally
> ½ teaspoon salt
> 2 tablespoons firmly packed light brown sugar
> 1 tablespoon water

In a medium-sized skillet, melt the butter over low heat. Add the plantains and sauté for 8 to 10 minutes on each side, until golden brown. Sprinkle with the salt, then add the brown sugar and water and continue cooking until the sugar is dissolved and the plantains are evenly coated. Serve immediately.

NOTE: Not to be eaten raw, plantains have the flavor and texture of something like a cross between potatoes and bananas. They're available in the supermarket produce section and are definitely worth checking out.

Special Occasion Salad

10 to 12 servings

Orzo is a nice change-of-pace pasta that's perfect for this dish, which comes from an old friend. She made it on special occasions and, boy, I couldn't wait for it!

½ pound orzo or Rosamarina pasta
1 can (20 ounces) pineapple chunks in their own
    juice, drained, and juice reserved
¾ cup sugar
3 tablespoons all-purpose flour
1 container (8 ounces) frozen whipped topping,
    thawed
1 can (11 ounces) mandarin oranges, drained
6 to 8 whole maraschino cherries

In a large saucepan, cook the pasta in boiling water according to package directions, for 15 to 18 minutes. Meanwhile, place the reserved pineapple juice in a small saucepan over medium heat; add the sugar and flour and stir until thickened. Set aside to cool. Drain the cooked pasta and set aside to cool. Place the cooled pasta in a large bowl and stir in the pineapple chunks and thickened sauce. Chill for 4 hours or overnight, then add the whipped topping and mandarin oranges, mixing well. Place in a large serving bowl and top with the cherries. Serve cold.

NOTE: Don't have whole maraschino cherries? No problem! Just add cherry or grape halves, or any other cut fresh fruit that'll add some fun color.

Waldorf Gelatin

5 to 6 servings

Do you love Waldorf salad but hate the last-minute work of putting it all together? Hooray! I found you a way to enjoy its great taste without the last-minute work!

> 1¼ cups apple juice, divided
> 1 package (4-serving size) strawberry-flavor
>   gelatin mix
> Ice cubes
> 1 cup peeled and finely chopped apple (about 1
>   medium-sized apple)
> 2 medium-sized bananas, sliced
> 2 tablespoons chopped pecans

In a small saucepan, bring ¾ cup of the apple juice to a boil. Place the gelatin in a large bowl and stir in the boiling apple juice for 2 minutes, or until completely dissolved. Place the remaining ½ cup apple juice in a 1-cup measuring cup and add enough ice to make 1 cup. Add to the gelatin, stirring until slightly thickened. Remove any remaining pieces of ice. Stir in the chopped apple, bananas, and pecans. Spoon into individual dessert dishes or a large serving bowl. Chill for 2 hours, or until firm.

NOTE: Don't have any bananas? Just add another apple instead.

Pineapple "Jiggles"

5 to 6 servings

Imagine carving canned pineapple right in front of the kids! Sound crazy? Well, this is a sure way to put smiles on those little faces, and magic on your table.

> 2 cans (20 ounces each) pineapple slices
> 1 package (4 serving size) lime-flavor gelatin mix

Open the pineapple cans cleanly and carefully drain the pineapple syrup, saving the syrup for another use and leaving the slices in the cans. Prepare the gelatin in a glass bowl according to the package directions. Let cool at room temperature for about 20 minutes. Pour half of the gelatin into the first can of pineapple slices. Place the handle of a wooden spoon into the center of the slices to loosen them so that the gelatin will flow between them. Repeat with the second can and remaining gelatin. Chill for 4 to 5 hours, until well set. When ready to serve, carefully cut open the bottom of each can and run a butter knife around the sides of each can; gently shake out the pineapple "rolls" and cut between each slice. Arrange the slices on a platter by themselves or place around cooked ham, chicken, or other dishes.

NOTE: Don't care for lime-flavored gelatin? Try it with any flavor you want.

Grapevine Salad

4 to 6 servings

Did you ever have a recipe so special that all your friends wanted to know where you got it? Well, this is one of those . . . and when they ask you where you got it, just tell them you "heard it through the grapevine."

> 2 eggs
> ½ cup orange juice
> 2 cups any type seedless grapes, cut in half
> ¼ cup maraschino cherries, cut in half
> ½ cup chopped walnuts
> 1 can (20 ounces) pineapple chunks, drained
> 2 medium-sized bananas, sliced

In a small saucepan over very low heat, cook the eggs and orange juice until slightly thickened, stirring constantly; set aside to cool. Meanwhile, in a medium-sized bowl, combine the remaining ingredients. Fold in the egg mixture until evenly combined and chill overnight to "marry" the flavors.

*NOTE: Remember, this is **your** recipe. Add a bit more nuts if you'd like, or maybe omit the cherries . . . Of course you know there are no rules.*

Harvest Apples and Pears

6 servings

Sometimes you want something homemade-yummy but need to take a shortcut . . . Well, this one has all the homemade taste you're looking for, and it's ready in a jiffy!

1 can (16 ounces) pear halves in syrup
1 jar (24 ounces) chunky-style applesauce
½ teaspoon ground cinnamon
Pinch of ground cloves
2 tablespoons honey

Drain the pears and save the juice for another use. Chop the pears and place in a large saucepan; add the remaining ingredients and cook over low heat for 10 to 15 minutes, until hot and bubbly. Serve hot, or cover and chill until ready to serve.

NOTE: What a great way to use up overripe or bruised fresh pears. Just remove the skins, core the pears, and chop as above.

Creamy Cranberry Creation

6 servings

We always had both gelatin and cranberries with our holiday meals, so now I've combined these two great memories into one terrific year-round side dish.

> 1 package (4-serving size) any flavor red gelatin mix
> 1 cup boiling water
> 1 can (16 ounces) whole-berry cranberry sauce
> 2 tablespoons orange juice
> ½ cup sour cream

In a medium-sized bowl, dissolve the gelatin in the boiling water. In a large bowl, break up the cranberry sauce into chunks with a fork until no large pieces are left. Stir in the orange juice, then the gelatin. Fold in the sour cream. Chill in the bowl or in a 3-cup gelatin mold for 2 to 3 hours, until firm. Serve right from the bowl or invert the mold over a large serving platter and unmold. Serve chilled.

NOTE: To unmold the gelatin, scrape a butter knife around the sides to loosen it and/or place a warm dish towel around the mold and turn the mold upside down on a serving platter that's at least I inch larger around than the mold.

Fruit Salsa:
The "Other" Salsa

about 3½ cups

This is like a relish or chutney—a yummy "something different" to tantalize your taste buds.

> 6 nectarines or peaches, pitted and cut into small
>   pieces
> ¾ cup raisins
> 1 cup firmly packed dark brown sugar
> ¾ cup cider vinegar
> ¼ cup finely chopped onions
> ¼ teaspoon ground ginger
> ¼ teaspoon cayenne pepper
> ¼ teaspoon salt

Place all the ingredients in a large saucepan. Bring to a boil, stirring constantly. Reduce the heat and simmer, uncovered, for 1 hour, stirring occasionally. Serve warm, or cover and chill until ready to serve.

NOTE: Great served warm or cold with cooked chicken, meat, or fish. Perfect for using leftover nectarines or peaches, it'll hold, covered, in the fridge for 1 to 2 weeks.

153

Fruit Festival

Tomorrow's Ambrosia

12 servings

Don't let the name of this fruit-filled fantasy fool ya', 'cause it's really simple . . . Mix it today, serve it tomorrow.

> 2 eggs, lightly beaten
> 4 tablespoons white vinegar
> 4 tablespoons sugar
> 2 tablespoons butter, softened
> 1 jar (10 ounces) maraschino cherries, drained and cut into halves
> 2 cups miniature marshmallows
> 1 can (20 ounces) pineapple chunks, drained
> 1 cup flaked coconut
> ½ pint heavy cream, whipped, or 1 container (8 ounces) frozen whipped topping, thawed

Place the eggs in the top of a double boiler (or in a stainless steel bowl over a saucepan of simmering water) and, over medium-low heat, add the vinegar and sugar and stir constantly until the mixture is thick and smooth. Remove from the heat, stir in the butter, and let cool. When the mixture is cool, fold in the cherries, marshmallows, pineapple, and coconut. Then fold in the whipped cream or whipped topping. Pour into a large serving bowl and chill, covered, for about 4 hours. Serve chilled.

NOTE: If you need a fancy dish for a special occasion, then pour the completed mixture into a 2-quart gelatin mold and refrigerate overnight. Before serving, unmold carefully onto a serving platter. If you don't have miniature marshmallows, use regular-sized marshmallows cut into quarters.

Index

broccoli (*continued*)
  and rice melt, 58
  snappy stir-fry, 102
buttermilk biscuits:
  potato pockets, 31
  vegetable rounds, 97
butternut squash, tropical, 96
butter potatoes, 26

C

cabbage:
  availability of, 86
  Bavarian, 107
  Chinese, 7
  everything coleslaw, 132
  "German" coleslaw, 137
  Napa, 7
  noodles and, 75
  salad, Asian, 17
  sweet-and-sour red, 111
  tropical coleslaw, 129
Caesar dressing, creamy, 21
canned foods:
  potatoes, 26
  vegetables, 84
cantaloupe:
  availability of, 142
  serving of, 141
capellini pasta, 79
carrot(s):
  autumn sweet potatoes, 45
  availability of, 86
  bake, 90
  cauliflower steamin' stir-fry, 104
  everything coleslaw, 132
  "German" coleslaw, 137
  pancakes, 109
  peppery, with dill, 105
  salad, "grate," 131
  tropical coleslaw, 129
cauliflower:
  availability of, 86
  confetti vegetable salad, 134
  steamin' stir-fry, 104
celery, availability of, 86
cheese:
  broiled garden tomatoes, 94
  carrot bake, 90
  creamy Caesar dressing, 21

curly Cheddar bake, 69
dressing, blue, 16
French onion pickups, 100
herbed mashed potatoes, 33
ivory peaches, 144
noodles, 'n' peas, 70
"ooh" gratin potatoes, 40
potato patties, 42
rice and broccoli melt, 58
salad toppers, 10
simple potato soufflé, 43
Southwestern layered rice, 59
tortellini, garlic, 76
true-blue potato salad, 47
vegetable rounds, 97
winter rice, 60
cherries:
  availability of, 142
  grapevine salad, 150
  Maui Maui rice, 62
  special occasion salad, 147
  tomorrow's ambrosia, 154
  warm honey walnut dressing, 18
chicory, 6, 7
chile(s):
  beans, Northern, 110
  New Mexican couscous, 119
Chinese cabbage, 7
  salad, 17
citrus stuffing, 120
coconut, in tomorrow's ambrosia, 154
coleslaw:
  everything, 132
  "German," 137
  tropical, 129
confetti salad:
  rice, 64
  vegetable, 134
cooking spray, nonstick vegetable, 1
corn:
  availability of, 86
  cooking of, 87–88
  New Mexican couscous, 119
  one-dish veggies, 89
  stuffing, spicy, 115
  Texas, 103
cornmeal, in Italian polenta, 123
couscous, New Mexican, 119

Index

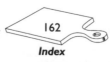

Mr. Food®

Can Help You Be A Kitchen Hero!

Let **Mr. Food**® make your life easier with

Quick, No-Fuss Recipes and Helpful Kitchen Tips for

Family Dinners   Soups and Salads   Pot Luck Dishes
Barbecues   Special Brunches   Unbelievable Desserts

...and that's just the beginning!

There are easy, updated versions of Mama's specialties in **Mr. Food**® *Cooks Like Mama*, new twists on American classics in **Mr. Food**® *Cooks Real American*, and scrumptious treats in **Mr. Food**® *Makes Dessert* and **Mr. Food**® *'s Favorite Cookies*. And now, with the incredibly simple **Mr. Food**® *'s Quick and Easy Side Dishes*, the barbecuing bonanza in **Mr. Food**® *Grills It All in a Snap*, and the gold mine of helpful hints in **Mr. Food**® *'s Fun Kitchen Tips and Shortcuts (and Recipes, Too!)*, **it's all here!** All of **Mr. Food**®**'s** recipes use readily-available ingredients, and can be made in no time! So, don't miss out! Join in on the fun!

It's so simple to share in all the
OOH IT'S SO GOOD!!™

✂--

TITLE	PRICE	QUANTITY	
A. **Mr. Food**® Cooks Like Mama	@ $12.95 ea.	x _____	= $_____
B. The **Mr. Food**® Cookbook, *OOH IT'S SO GOOD!!*™	@ $12.95 ea.	x _____	= $_____
C. **Mr. Food**® Cooks Chicken	@ $ 9.95 ea.	x _____	= $_____
D. **Mr. Food**® Cooks Pasta	@ $ 9.95 ea.	x _____	= $_____
E. **Mr. Food**® Makes Dessert	@ $ 9.95 ea.	x _____	= $_____
F. **Mr. Food**® Cooks Real American	@ $14.95 ea.	x _____	= $_____
G. **Mr. Food**®**'s** Favorite Cookies	@ $11.95 ea.	x _____	= $_____
H. **Mr. Food**®**'s** Quick and Easy Side Dishes	@ $11.95 ea.	x _____	= $_____
I. **Mr. Food**® Grills It All in a Snap	@ $11.95 ea.	x _____	= $_____
J. **Mr. Food**®**'s** Fun Kitchen Tips and Shortcuts (and Recipes, Too!)	@ $11.95 ea.	x _____	= $_

Send payment to: **Mr. Food**®
P.O. Box 696
Holmes, PA 19043

Book Total $_____

Name_____

+$2.95 Postage & Handling *First Copy* AND
$1 Ea. Add'l. Copy (Canadian Orders Add Add'l. $2.00 *Per Copy*) $_____

Street_____

Subtotal $_____

City_____State_____Zip_____

Less $1.00 per book if ordering 3 or more books with this order $-_____

Method of Payment: ☐Check or Money Order Enclosed
☐ Credit Card: ☐ Visa ☐ MasterCard: Expiration Date _____
Signature_____

Add Applicable Sales Tax (FL Residents Only) $_____

Total in U.S. Funds $_____

Account #:

☐☐☐☐☐☐☐☐☐☐☐☐☐☐☐☐☐☐☐

Please allow 4 to 6 weeks for delivery.   BKI1